CW01188821

J. Graeme Bruce

WORKHORSES OF THE
LONDON UNDERGROUND

Capital Transport

First published 1987

ISBN 0 904711 87 0

Published by Capital Transport Publishing
38 Long Elmes, Harrow Weald, Middlesex

Printed by KPC Print, Ashford, Kent

Bound by Standard Book Binding,
39 Standard Road, London NW10

© J. Graeme Bruce 1987

Acknowledgements

The information contained in this book has been collected over many years and has only been made possible by the help and interest of many people, all of them colleagues, both active and retired, in the affairs of London Transport. Only a few whose help has been of considerable value can be mentioned, but there were many others. Ken King, former Superintendent of Traffic, was generous with his encyclopaedic knowledge of Traffic Circulars and their contents; Gordon Hafter recently retired as Director of Mechanical Engineering; Bill Tonkyn, now Rolling Stock Technical Officer; and the late Harry Clarke, who was a Divisional Rolling Stock Engineer, were all associated with the Author in responsibility for the maintenance of the vast bulk of the vehicles mentioned in the text; Andrew Gilkes' interest in the Rolling Stock Records and the vehicle numbering system has been of considerable help. I have also made a lot of use of information culled from the archives at Acton by Piers Connor. Finally, Brian Hardy and Bob Greenaway require special recognition for the generous provision of photographs from their collections and for ensuring that some eight years away from my active participation in the events, the continued development of the miscellaneous fleet has not been neglected.

The extensive fleet lists are the work of Brian Hardy. In spite of the official help, the opinions expressed are those of the author and not necessarily those of London Regional Transport.

Harrow, January 1987   J. GRAEME BRUCE

Photographic Credits

J. Graeme Bruce collection C186.
Dr A.W. Gilks Piccadilly motor car 3282.
R.J. Greenaway L94 at Barbican, Met Loco No. 15, 1935 stock articulated unit, L84, FB578, G663, TLC2, TCC2, TCC3, L133, TRC666.
R.J. Greenaway collection Met Loco No. 93, L30, L91, L1 and L5, Met Loco No. 10, L26, L28, RG207.
Brian Hardy L11, L13A/B, L56, DL83, L130/1, L126/7, L146/7, B559, PC855, PC858, F350, HW433, RW490, RG802/3, G662, VKR05 tamper, PU0716 tamper, TRC912, TCC1.
D.W.K. Jones C604.
London Underground Railway Society L10, L16, F329, District Railway Brake Coach.
Photomatic L48, L31, L34, L90.
Real Photographs CLR No. 2, GCP&B battery loco No. 2B, Gauging car on 1904 underframe.

Photographs not otherwise credited are copyright LRT.

The cover illustrations are by D.W.K. Jones, R.J. Greenaway and Brian Hardy.

CONTENTS

STEAM LOCOMOTIVES	**4**
ELECTRIC LOCOMOTIVES	**14**
BATTERY LOCOMOTIVES	**26**
DIESEL LOCOMOTIVES	**37**
BALLAST & PILOT MOTORS	**40**
WORKS & MISCELLANEOUS VEHICLES	**48**
TRAVELLING CRANES	**60**
PERMANENT WAY VEHICLES	**69**
AUTUMN & WINTER WORKING	**80**
SERVICE STOCK LIST	**88**

Frontispiece **Two former Metropolitan Railway locomotives retained by London Transport 'on shed' at Neasden. The 0-6-0ST was Met No. 101 built by Peckett of Bristol in 1897. The 0-4-4T No. 44 was formerly No. 1 in its Met days, being built at Neasden in 1898 to replace the A class locomotive of the same number which was withdrawn after an accident.**

STEAM LOCOMOTIVES

On the 10th January 1863 the first section of the Metropolitan Railway was opened between Paddington and Farringdon, the first underground railway in the world. Sir John Fowler, the engineer of the project, devised a fireless locomotive in which the water was heated to produce steam by the use of white hot bricks, pre-heated external to the locomotive, and Robert Stephenson and Co Ltd, built a prototype.

This locomotive was of the 2-4-0 wheel arrangement and became known as Fowlers Ghost. It was a genuine attempt to avoid the production of smoke and fumes in the confined space of the underground railway tunnels, but does not seem to have had much success and was eventually sold in 1865 and scrapped.

The Great Western Railway originally had a considerable financial interest in the building of the Metropolitan Railway and Daniel Gooch, their famous Locomotive Superintendent, designed a broad gauge condensing tank locomotive of a similar wheel arrangement to Fowler's Ghost. Vulcan Foundry constructed six and Kitson and Co a further six and it was with these 12 locomotives that the Metropolitan Railway service was opened. In the early days, the water tanks of the locomotives were emptied at Farringdon Street and replenished with cold water to improve the condensing on the return journey.

The Great Western Railway at this time had a rail gauge of 7ft 0¼ins and the Metropolitan Railway was originally constructed to dual gauge, a third rail being laid to provide the standard gauge of 4ft 8½ins.

A disagreement arose in August 1863 with the Great Western Railway who then withdrew their locomotives and rolling stock. Arrangements were quickly made for the Great Northern Railway, with whom a junction had been established at Kings Cross, to supply the rolling stock and motive power for the service but with standard gauge vehicles. When this service was introduced many derailments occurred because maintenance of the third rail for the narrower gauge had been neglected while the service had been maintained by broad gauge vehicles

Standard gauge working began on 10th August 1863 but this was not the end of broad gauge trains working through the tunnels, because on 1st October 1863 the Great Western inaugurated through business trains from Windsor to Farringdon. In addition, when the Hammersmith and City Railway began operating as a Metropolitan and Great Western Railway joint venture, this too was of mixed gauge and broad gauge trains worked between Farringdon and Hammersmith from 13th June 1864.

The broad gauge lines on the Underground were taken out of use, however, on 1st March 1869. Subsequently the Metropolitan Railway was operated by its own locomotives of standard gauge, obtained from Beyer Peacock of Gorton, Manchester. A total of 120 of this original type of 4-4-0T locomotive was built by 1886, sixty-six for the Metropolitan Railway and 54 for the second underground railway, the Metropolitan District Railway.

The Metropolitan District Railway, between South Kensington and Westminster, was opened to traffic on 24th December 1868 and was worked initially by the the Metropolitan.

The service required only eight locomotives but by 1871 there were 12 trains per hour between South Kensington and Mansion House, half of them from Moorgate by the Metropolitan Railway and half of them from West Brompton operated by the District. The District then obtained its own locomotives from Beyer Peacock to the same basic design as the Metropolitan ones, and began working on its own account from 3rd July 1871.

The two groups of locomotives were generally similar in design but had a number of detail differences. The Metropolitan Railway from about 1870 used the automatic vacuum brake after having extensively tried the first ever continuous brake, the Clark-Webb chain brake, on their passenger trains.

A few years later, in 1875, the District adopted the Westinghouse air brake, which at first was non-automatic but after 1879 became 'automatic'. After electrification the Metropolitan rolling stock was provided with either vacuum or Westinghouse braking systems on different electric trains but the Metropolitan steam trains always used the vacuum brake. The two systems were of course incompatible and only locomotives where it was considered necessary were dual equipped. The District never had this problem having adopted the Westinghouse brake as standard even for their steam stock.

On the Circle service, which was jointly worked, it was usual for the Metropolitan to operate the 'Outer' rail service while the District worked the 'Inner Rail' with some balancing mileage by Metropolitan trains because the larger part of the track mileage was owned by the Metropolitan Railway.

The Metropolitan Railway went on to purchase and build a number of types of steam locomotive for general work but the District Railway, during the steam era, relied entirely on the 4-4-0 Beyer Peacock tank engine for passenger trains.

One of the original Beyer Peacock 4-4-0 Met locos in the Metropolitan Railway lined livery. Built in 1864, No. 16 is shown after its second reboilering in 1895 when it was given a new chimney and the dome was moved rearwards on the boiler. Note the lack of a cab roof, which crews eschewed when the engines worked the Circle service.

One of the original batch of Beyer Peacock locomotives built in 1871 for the Metropolitan District Railway. The air brake compressor mounted at the side of the boiler and the compressed air storage tank underneath the coal bunker can be clearly seen. The District was the first railway to use the Westinghouse brake in England and got very favourable contract prices as a result. Most of these 4-4-0 locomotives were scrapped by 1907.

The original 54 District Railway locomotives were constructed as follows:—

1871	Nos. 1-24
1876	Nos. 25-30
1881	Nos. 31-36
1883	Nos. 37-42
1884	Nos. 43-48
1886	Nos. 49-54

After electrification, the Metropolitan Railway operated a considerable fleet of steam locomotives for passenger and goods train working beyond its electrified territory. Electric locomotives were obtained to work these within the electrified area, so that a change of motive power was necessary where the electrified tracks ended. At first, from 1st November 1906, this was arranged at Wembley Park but the locomotive change was moved to Harrow-on-the-Hill on 19th July 1908 when the station rebuilding there had been completed. The station had been rebuilt to provide four platforms instead of two, with coal staithes and locomotive sidings accessible to the through lines so that the locomotive changes for the Metropolitan trains could be conveniently arranged with the minimum of delay.

Following the extension of the electrification to Rickmansworth, the locomotive change was moved on 5th January 1925 from Harrow-on-the-Hill to that station, where it remained until the need for changing locomotives ceased on 9th September 1961.

After electrification, the District put up for disposal all its steam locomotives except six. These were retained in working order beyond the operation of its last steam passenger train which occurred on 5th November 1905. Forty-eight locomotives were offered for sale for the total scrap value of £15,000.

Of the six Beyer Peacock locomotives retained on the District only two, Nos. 33 and No. 34, were in fact still serviceable in 1909. Both these locomotives had been built in 1881 and were retained to handle ballast and works trains. They were required to perform shunting duties in Lillie Bridge Depot and to work down into Kensington goods yard. It is not now clear why these two locomotives were selected for retention rather than two from the last batch which were at least five years younger but they may have had recent expensive boiler repairs which rendered them more reliable.

Locomotive No. 33 was scrapped in 1925 and was replaced by the purchase of a similar locomotive from the Metropolitan Railway. This was numbered 22 in the Metropolitan fleet, but when transferred to the District was renumbered 35. This locomotive was of course fitted with vacuum brake equipment and retained this while working on the District. District locomotive No. 34 was not fitted with a cab until 1927. Both these locomotives were retained mainly for shunting duties at Lillie Bridge until 1932. The numbers were prefixed with an L after the delivery of the Hunslet locomotives in 1931 when the new numbering scheme was introduced.

5

The fate of the Metropolitan Railway locomotives was more complex. After electrification of the Circle Line, some 32 of the Beyer Peacock locomotives were sold and these had all gone by 1907. As the Uxbridge Line was virtually an entirely new service requiring electric trains, it did not involve the immediate replacement and disposal of any steam locomotives. A further batch of eight had, however, been disposed of by 1913. By 1925, when the electrification reached Rickmansworth, a further scrapping programme left only five of the Beyer Peacock tank locomotives (Nos. 23, 27, 41, 48 and 49) working. Nos. 23 and 41 were the locomotives normally used on the Brill branch, but after this was closed, all but No. 23 were finally withdrawn in 1936. No. 23 had by then been renumbered L45 in the London Transport numbering scheme, and was used only for shunting in Neasden Yard. In 1948 it became necessary to withdraw it from active service when extensive boiler repairs were required. It was the sole survivor of an outstandingly successful locomotive type used to work the original sections of the Underground system, and it was therefore retained for preservation. These locomotives when in working condition, weighed 46½ tons and had cylinders 17 inches in diameter with stroke of 24 inches.

Co-operation with main line railway companies also had an effect on the history of the steam locos. The Metropolitan had reached Chesham by 8th July 1889 and a through service was established a year later and a through G.C.R. passenger service to the new terminal at Marylebone began on 15th March 1899 from the north. On the 2nd April 1906 the Metropolitan & Great Central Joint Committee was formed to manage the lines north of Harrow, but the Metropolitan Railway continued to work the local services. London Transport took over this operation from its formation in 1933 until 1st November 1937, when the passenger service beyond Rickmansworth and all goods workings were transferred to the London & North Eastern Railway.

The steam locomotives owned by the Metropolitan Railway at the time of the formation of London Transport numbered 36, but this number was soon reduced to 32.

The Metropolitan & Great Central Joint Committee continued to function after the formation of London Transport but upon nationalisation in 1948 the lines to Aylesbury, Chesham and Watford were allocated to London Transport although British Railways continued to provide the steam locomotives beyond the change point at Rickmansworth. In 1961 however, the lines beyond Amersham were transferred to the control of British Railways and through trains from Baker Street beyond that point ceased.

The reconstruction of Neasden Works as an electric rolling stock running depot under the 1935/40 programme, precluded the provision of improved facilities for the maintenance of a large fleet of steam locomotives. An agreement was reached with the London & North Eastern Railway, operative from 1st November 1937, for that railway to take over the provision of the steam locomotives for all the revenue work, both passenger and goods, leaving only a small fleet of steam locomotives in the possession of London Transport for railway maintenance work. A new small running shed for the maintenance of steam locomotives was provided as part of the facilities at Neasden Depot but the heavy maintenance of all London Transport steam locomotives was then undertaken at the facilities already available at Lillie Bridge. The London & North Eastern Railway at this time took over 18 steam locomotives, 252 goods wagons and 13 brake vans from London Transport, all of which had been inherited from the Metropolitan Railway. London Transport retained 14 steam locomotives for non revenue work such as muck-shifting, permanent way work and power house shunting.

The locomotives sold to the London & North Eastern Railway on 1st November 1937 are listed at the foot of this page.

Four of the E class 0-4-4T locomotives were among those retained in London Transport service. This class of locomotive had been designed by T.F. Clark, the Metropolitan Locomotive Superintendent in 1896. Three of the original 7 locomotives were built at Neasden while the other four were constructed by Hawthorn Leslie. The whole class was constructed between 1896 and 1901.

L44, which very curiously had been Metropolitan loco No. 1 (the second to have used that number), was built at Neasden in 1898. After withdrawal, it was purchased in 1964 by the London Railway Preservation Society and is among the vehicles now at Quainton Road under the auspices of the Buckinghamshire Railway Centre. This locomotive in fact hauled the first passenger train from Harrow to Uxbridge in July 1904 before the electrification was completed. At the Centenary Exhibition at Neasden in May 1963, L44 hauled the 'Chesham' shuttle passenger coaches.

L46 (formerly Metropolitan No. 77) built at Neasden in 1896 was withdrawn in 1962 and cut up for scrap at the same location that winter. The two other locomotives of this class which had been retained by London Transport were L47 and L48 (Metropolitan No. 80 and No. 81 respectively), built by Hawthorn Leslie in 1900. L47 was withdrawn in 1941 but L48 lasted until 1963.

Locomotives of this class had originally been built for passenger working on the Aylesbury Line but after 1937, they were used on ballast trains mainly out of Neasden Yard.

The four F class 0-6-2 tank locomotives built by the Yorkshire Engine Co were also retained by London Transport in 1937. When built, these locomotives had not been provided with steam heating equipment and had therefore been confined to goods working.

The Metropolitan numbers had been 90-93 and with LT renumbering became L49-L52 respectively. L52

Locomotives sold to the LNER, 1/11/37

Type	Class	Met Nos.	LNE Classification	LNE Nos.	Total
0-6-4T	G	94-97	M2	6154-6157	4
4-4-4T	H	103-110	H2	6415-6422	6
2-6-4T	K	111-116	L2	6158-6163	8

All these locomotives were reconditioned at Stratford works before taking up duty with their new owners.

Above **L48**, built in 1900 by Hawthorn Leslie and originally Met E class loco No. 81, lasted on ballast train duties until 1963, working out of Neasden. The seven engines of this class were originally constructed for Aylesbury passenger services. Note the tripcock safety device between the coupled wheels.

L52 awaiting scrapping at Neasden in 1963. Originally Metropolitan Railway locomotive 93, it was an 0-6-2 tank engine built by Yorkshire Engine Company in 1901, mainly for passenger train duties on the Aylesbury line. This F class locomotive remained in active service until 1962 on ballast train workings.

The same locomotive in Metropolitan Railway livery approaching Harrow-on-the-Hill with a Met brake van.

L53, one of two Peckett saddle tank 0-6-0 locomotives originally built in 1897 and numbered 101 in the Metropolitan Railway fleet, was used for shunting duties at Neasden and at Finchley Road goods yard where an interchange with the Midland Railway had been established. The Locomotive was withdrawn from active duty in 1960.

was not withdrawn from active service until 1962. It was retained for use in the Centenary Celebrations at Neasden in 1963 and was cut up at Neasden during 1964 for scrap. The other three were withdrawn from duty in 1957/58.

Two small 0-6-0 saddle tank engines were obtained by the Metropolitan Railway in 1897/9 from Peckett and Sons for yard shunting at Finchley Road and Harrow goods yards. Finchley Road was an important interchange point for goods traffic having an access track to the Midland Railway goods yard. These two locomotives were numbered 101 and 102 by the Metropolitan, but later became L53 and L54 when renumbered by London Transport. From 1937 until withdrawn in 1960/61 they were used for shunting in Neasden Yard, being especially useful on the Power Station duties which required the feeding of coal trains into the coal hoists and removal of the ash and slurry wagons for disposal of waste material. L54 was latterly engaged on shunting duties at Lillie Bridge.

The first steam locomotives to be given numbers prefixed by an 'L' were those ordered from the Hunslet Engine Co. of Leeds by the District Railway in 1931. They were given the numbers L30 and L31 right from the start which they retained all their working life. They were 0-6-0 tank locomotives required for ballast train working and shunting at Lillie Bridge.

Although these locomotives had driving wheels 4ft 2ins in diameter, they could work under restricted loading gauge conditions as the chimney height was only 12ft 3ins from rail level and the footplate had a restricted width of 8ft 8ins. In working order the locomotives weighed 44 tons and had a length of 34 feet over buffers. They carried 1½ tons of coal and 1,200 gallons of water. The locomotives had outside cylinders 16ins by 24ins, supplied with steam at 200psi through Walschaerts valve gear and could exert a tractive effort of 20,500lbs. They spent most of their life on shunting duties at Lillie Bridge yard and on stores trains to and from Acton Works and Ealing Common Depot, with occasional ballast train trips on the District Railway to East Ham.

One of two 0-6-0 tank locomotives built by Hunslet for the District Railway in 1931. They were the last steam locomotives built specifically for any of the Underground railways and spent most of their time working out of Lillie Bridge on works trains. L30 is shown outside the steam shed at Lillie Bridge shortly after its delivery.

The two Hunslet 0-6-0T locomotives lasted until 1964. Here L31 is seen at Lillie Bridge in the London Transport livery.

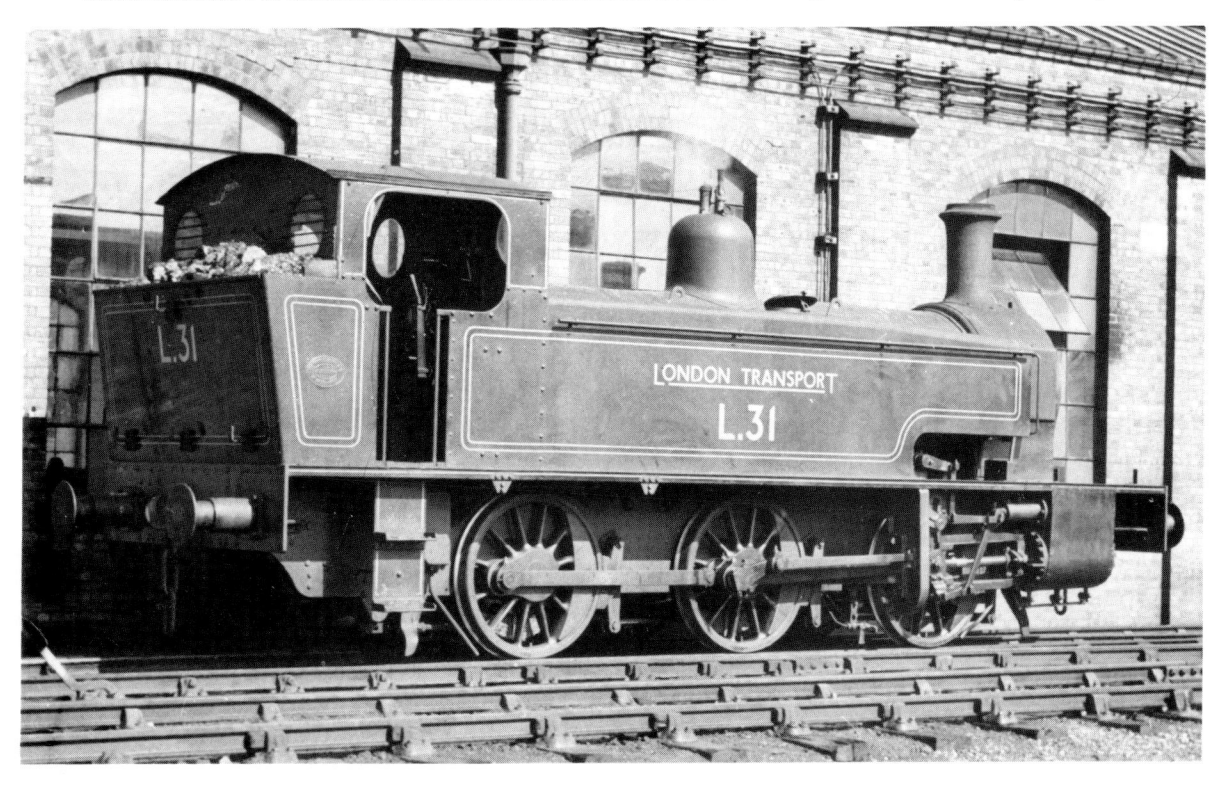

Although the tube railways had atmospheric difficulties in using steam locomotives for work in tunnel sections, there were a number of such locomotives built to tube loading gauge.

The Hunslet Engine Co. of Leeds designed in 1899 two such locomotives for the Central London Railway, to work in the confined space of a tube tunnel with a diameter of 11ft 6ins. Although the cabs of these locomotives were wide they had very little headroom.

These engines, which were given the numbers 1 and 2, were used before the opening of the line to take into the tunnels the fixed equipment necessary to establish operations after the main civil engineering contractors had completed their construction work. Subsequently, they were mainly used above ground, shunting coal wagons for Wood Lane power house from the reception roads which branched off the West London Extension Railway. They were oil fired so that they could be operated by one man, a fireman not being normally necessary.

Condensing arrangements were provided so that they could, on occasions, operate into the running tunnels. The side tanks could store 1,000 gallons of water purely for this purpose. Other tanks to the rear could carry a further 250 gallons which provided the boiler feed water. The bunker fuel tanks carried 50 gallons of oil, but the grate was arranged so that coal could be used, and when working above ground, ¾ ton of coal was carried. The locomotive cylinders were placed inside the main frames to improve the clearance for tunnel working. These cylinders were 14½ins × 18ins and were supplied with steam at 150psi, giving a tractive effort of 12,300lbs. The wheel arrangement was 0-6-0, with wheels of 3ft 3ins diameter, the middle pair of which had no flanges so that the locomotives could negotiate curves of 150 feet radius. The wheel layout was symmetrical, with a wheelbase of 17 feet.

These two Central London steam locomotives were scrapped in 1923 although the power station at Wood Lane did not cease working until 18th March 1928.

Central London Railway steam locomotive No. 2 built by Hunslet in 1899 for the equipment work associated with the construction of the Central London Railway. The double buffer arrangement enabled coupling to be made with the link and pin drawgear of that railway's rolling stock as well as with the RCH type couplings on main line wagons.

L34 at Drapers Field, Leyton in 1947. This locomotive was originally owned by the City & South London Railway Company and was built by Kerr Stuart in 1922.

In 1922 Kerr Stuart and Co built a small saddle tank locomotive of 0-4-2 wheel arrangement, which was known as the 'Brazil'. It was owned by the City & South London Railway not the London Electric Railway, and was used for equipping the Morden extension. This locomotive was constructed to dimensions which enabled it to work through tube tunnels, the height from rail level to the top of the chimney being only 9ft 6ins. It weighed 14 tons in full working order, carrying 15cwts of coal and 270 gallons of water. The cylinders were 9ins × 15 ins with driving wheels only 2ft 6ins in diameter. The maximum working steam pressure was 160psi and at 85 per cent cut off a tractive effort of 6,500lbs was attainable. The locomotive was given the number L34 in 1930 and during the construction work in connection with the Piccadilly extension to Cockfosters it was stationed at Arnos Grove and Cockfosters. Subsequently it went to Drapers Field, Leyton for the eastern extension of the Central Line. In 1949, when this work was completed, it was withdrawn and scrapped.

Because of the difficulty of maintaining a mixed fleet of steam locomotives of increasing age, arrangements were made in 1956 to hire two Western Region 0-6-0 pannier tank engines to replace the two F class locomotives L49 and L51. The first locomotive (WR No. 7711) was transferred in October 1956, repainted in LT livery and renumbered L90 by January 1957. This locomotive had been built by Kerr Stuart in 1930. The second vehicle was WR No. 5752, which had been built at Swindon in 1929; she was repainted and renumbered L91 later in 1957.

L90 at Neasden in 1958. It was built by Kerr Stuart & Company in 1930 and numbered 7711 in the BR Western Region fleet before being sold to LT in 1956. L90 was replaced in 1961 by another Western Region locomotive which was given the same LT number.

These locomotives were found to be very successful and very suitable for duty on the London Transport surface lines with limited clearances. This class of locomotive was the best for the purpose as the later models of Western Region pannier tank engines were built to a larger loading gauge. It was agreed that these two trial locomotives would be replaced by fully overhauled engines and that a further number of similar locomotives would be purchased, with the running maintenance being undertaken by London Transport but with the Western Region undertaking any major repairs. The Western Region had surplus steam locomotives in good repair at this time because of the intensive dieselisation programme.

It was arranged that a further nine locomotives would be provided between 1958 and 1963. Meanwhile, 5752 and 7711 continued to work until November 1960 and October 1961 respectively, when they were replaced by 7760 (which took over the number L90) and 5757 (which acquired the number L91).

7760 was built at the North British Locomotive Works in Glasgow in 1930 and 5757 at Swindon in 1929. L90 together with L94 acquired later, formerly Great Western locomotives 7760 and 7752 respectively, were subsequently purchased by the Standard Gauge Steam Trust at Tyseley near Birmingham and repainted in Great Western Railway livery. L90 had on this occasion to be transferred off London Transport property by road.

In 1958 two further locomotives were obtained; 5786, which became L92, was built by the Great Western at Swindon and 7779, which became L93, by Armstrong Whitworth in 1930. L92 was subsequently sold to the Worcester Locomotive Preservation Society when the locomotive was taken out of service by London Transport in 1969. In 1964, L93 was the first Western Region type engine to be fitted with sleet brushes for use on the Wimbledon Line for ice and snow clearance under winter conditions.

The North British built locomotive 7752 was acquired in 1959, becoming L94 and in 1961 two more, 5764 (Great Western built) and 7741 (North British built) joined the fleet becoming L95 and L96.

L95 was the first of the Pannier tank engines to be fitted with a snow plough specially adapted for this type. The snow plough was given the number 1 and because it had to be held clear of the rails to accommodate the vertical rise under track curvature conditions it proved to be useful only in a very heavy snow fall, when the train service had in fact ceased. This was a very rare condition in the London area and this facility, tested in December 1962, was never actually used in a real situation.

The steam locomotive fleet was allowed to increase in total to 13 at this time in order to enable the Metropolitan four-tracking project to be serviced by additional works and equipping trains. This was achieved by the purchase of two further North British built locomotives, numbered 7749 and 7739, becoming L97 and L98. The last two Western Region steam locomotives acquired by London Transport (in mid-1963) were 7715, built by Kerr Stuart, and 5775 built at Swindon. No. 7715 became L99 but 5775 was numbered L89, at the beginning of the numerical series allocated to steam locomotives, to avoid using '100' which was already used on one of the electric sleet locomotives. These last two were obtained to enable

L91 (ex Western Region 5752) at Lillie Bridge in 1958. It was built at Swindon in 1929 and acquired by London Transport in 1957, being replaced by a similar locomotive in 1960.

L94 undergoing its last overhaul at Ealing Common depot in February 1971. This was the only steam locomotive to be lifted on these jacks provided for overhauling battery locos.

L30 and L31, which had been retained in active service until after the centenary display at Neasden in 1963, to be withdrawn. L99 was eventually sold to the London Railway Preservation Society and subsequently became part of the Quainton Railway Society collection (now Buckinghamshire Railway Centre). L89 was sold to the Keighley and Worth Valley Railway Preservation Society in 1970 and has been preserved in London Transport livery.

With the opening of the first part of the Victoria Line on 1st September 1968, the new battery locomotives purchased for the intensive commissioning work on that line were released, and this enabled a reappraisal of the motive power needs for works trains to be made. The result of this reappraisal was that the days of the steam locomotives in active service were numbered and L96 became the first of the fleet of Western Region locomotives owned by London Transport to be withdrawn.

The last three steam locomotives to remain operational with London Transport were L90, L94 and L95, which were not withdrawn until 1971. The last regular work undertaken by the steam locomotives was the haulge of the Croxley tip muck trains from Neasden and of the Acton Works stores train from Lillie Bridge, usually conveying new steel tyres and other heavy material. The Acton Works steam train ceased to operate in February 1971, and subsequently the Croxley tip trains were powered by battery locomotives.

The last 'revenue' type of duty performed by a steam engine was on the morning of 4th June 1971 when L90 was provided to bring a crane from Lillie Bridge to Neasden. The trip was marred by this locomotive 'dropping' the fusable plug at Harrow. This is one of the most serious types of failure that can occur to a

L95 at Neasden in 1963, fitted with the experimental snowplough. This device was not entirely successful because the plough had to be high above the running rails so that it could clear the conductor rails.

steam locomotive since it renders it completely immobile as a safeguard from an explosion or boiler blow back. The train arrived at Neasden ignominiously behind battery locomotives which had been despatched to rescue it.

The actual last day of steam operation was in fact 6th June 1971 when the event was celebrated by the running of a steam hauled train of engineering vehicles, specially marshalled for the occasion, from Moorgate in the City to Neasden Depot where a special display of rolling stock was arranged open to the public.

The special train consisted of locomotive L94, brake vans B582 and B557, rail wagon RW473, flat wagon F348, hopper wagon HW428, six ton diesel electric crane C617, jib carrier J688 and cable wagon F347. On arrival at Neasden Depot these vehicles were put on display. So ended the steam era on London Transport.

The last steam train on the London Underground, L94, on a commemorative run between Moorgate and Neasden on 16th June 1971. It is seen at Barbican.

Electric Locomotives

The City & South London Railway (originally the City of London & Southwark Subway, incorporated in 1884) was one of the first electric railways and certainly the first deep level (or tube) electric railway in the world. It was formally opened, between King William Street in the City of London and Stockwell on the south side of the River Thames, by the Prince of Wales (later to become King Edward VII) on 4th November 1890, but was not opened to the public until 18th December 1890.

It was originally designed for cable traction but in the initial stage of its construction it was decided that electricity would be used instead. The original tunnels north of Elephant & Castle were 10ft 2ins in diameter while those south of Elephant & Castle to Stockwell were constructed to a diameter of 10ft 6ins. This difference arose because the speed of haulage south of Elephant was to be over 12mph while north of this the speed was to be restricted to 10mph and it was thought that greater dynamic clearance was desirable with the operation at higher speed.

The track gauge was standard at 4ft 8½ins, provided by flat bottomed rail spiked to cross sleepers, without any ballast. The conductor rail was provided between the running rails, being of flat inverted channel sections with the collecting surface one inch below running rail level and not in the centre of the track. This rail, supported on glass insulators was placed 1ft 3ins from the left hand running rail looking north. Wooden ramps were provided to lift the collector shoes over the running rails at points and crossings. A plank walkway was laid in the other 'half' of the 'four foot' way.

The collector shoes were dished cast iron plates approximately 10ins square and at some locations movable bridges were provided, operated by point rodding, to ensure that the collector shoes cleared the running rails at crossings. This arrangement allowed maximum clearance for the gearless traction motors fitted to the locomotives, which were among the first electric locomotives in the world. This clearance also allowed the link and pin coupling connecting the locomotive to the carriages to be set low.

A depot was located at Stockwell, containing a repair shop and carriage shed as well as a generating station. The shed was connected to the running lines by means of a ramp which had a 1 in 3½ slope. The locomotives and carriages were pulled up this incline by a chain attached to a winding engine. The vehicles were moved about the depot by means of ropes and capstans provided with steam power from the power house. The incline was virtually replaced by the installation in 1906 of a 20 ton Waygood hydraulic lift which could take a carriage or a locomotive with less manual work and greater safety than the incline.

On 25th February 1900 the line was extended north to Moorgate Street and the original King William Street terminal abandoned. Later in the same year, on 3rd June, an extension to Clapham Common was opened. All these extensions were constructed with tunnels 10ft 6ins in diameter. The railway reached its maximum length of 7¼ miles on 12th May 1907 with the opening of the line to Euston.

When the line was first opened, the fleet of locomotives consisted of 14 machines built by Mather & Platt Ltd, of Manchester, only one of which had geared motors. The others had two motors constructed on the axles and connected in permanent series controlled by a rheostat with 26 contacts. Subsequently, additional locomotives were required as the line was extended and the later locomotives were provided with axle-hung nose-suspended motors connected in series parallel.

Originally, the locomotives, although being provided with a compressed air brake, were not provided with compressors. Twin air pumps were located in the power station maintaining a supply of compressed air at 80psi to Stockwell Station for charging the two air cylinders carried on the locomotives. These two reservoirs were recharged from this air main, at the end of each round trip. The fully charged reservoirs contained sufficient air to enable a total of 42 stops by the straight Westinghouse air brake; since initially there were only six stations, this was considered to be an adequate provision. However, after the line was extended, for safety reasons the locomotives were fitted with compressors, and the air main system abandoned.

The power distribution system adopted was that which had already found favour, particularly in America, for lighting systems from direct current power houses and called the 'three wire system'. Basically, this provided two 500 volt generators connected in series so that there was 1000 volts between the outer wires, but 500 volts between each and the centre point. In other words the system provided 500 volts positive to earth and 500 volts negative to earth when the neutral wire was earthed. As long as the two sections had a common earth, considerable advantage was obtained, by a reduction in the transmission losses by voltage drop, since the current could be considered to do twice the work for virtually the same loss in the transmission. The northbound line was placed in one section and the southbound in the other, with the terminal stations entirely within one or other section with a gap in the conductor rails sufficient to prevent a short arising between the two sections.

In 1913 the City & South London Railway came under the control of the Underground Group, who then promoted a Bill in Parliament to enlarge the tunnels to bring them into line with the standard adopted by the London Electric Railway and to provide a junction with that railway at Euston.

The reconstruction work did not commence until 1922 and it was planned that it should be achieved without closing down the train service. However, on 9th August 1922 the section between Moorgate and Euston was closed down completely but a train service at a reduced level was maintained between Moorgate and Clapham Common. Works trains taking in new equipment and removing the spoil from the City & South London tunnels were placed in position each night while the service was restored each day. The work's trains were hauled by one or other of the electric locomotives and the wagons were constructed from passenger cars no longer required because the service had been reduced. One or two of these cars were converted to battery carrying vehicles to provide power to the electric locomotives when current was discharged so that the works and muck trains could still be moved. One section between Oval and Stockwell where the working had to be carried out in compressed air because of water bearing soil, had a single line passenger operation arranged while one or other tunnel was being worked on. This in itself ensured a service reduction. However, on 27th November 1923, a serious mishap occurred south of Borough, after the restart of traffic, due to a gravel run into the tunnels. The service was subsequently abandoned and the traffic was transferred for many months to a bus service specially provided. The London General Omnibus Company allocated a special fleet of buses for the service, painted a distinctive blue and cream colour, and which only picked up and set down passengers at the railway stations.

A 50 foot heading about 4ft in diameter was opened up between the Piccadilly Line and the City & South London at King's Cross to enable rails in particular and other track material to be taken into the part to be rebuilt. In no other way could rails longer than 30ft be taken into the tunnel, since the hydraulic hoist at Stockwell, which had replaced the inclined tunnel, restricted the access. Parliamentary powers obtained for the rebuilding included a rail connection between the Piccadilly Line and the City & South London at King's Cross for engineering (not traffic) requirements and this was subsequently brought into use on 27th March 1927.

The enlargement of the City and South London tunnels from the original size to 11ft 8¼ins diameter, which had become the Underground standard, was achieved by re-using the old segments and inserting additional 'distance' pieces. The design size of the

A modified City & South London passenger car converted to take batteries to supply the modified locos for muck trains for the widening of C&SLR tunnels. Note the air brake hose at roof level and the connectors for the battery supply to the loco resting on the end platform.

Underground tunnel had in fact been 11ft 6ins, but it was subsequently decided to reduce the depth of the flanges of the iron segments which were bolted together and the working size of the tunnel was thus increased to 11ft 8¼ins while the actual bored tunnel remained unchanged. This decision actually determined the size of all subsequent new tube bores built until the construction of the Victoria Line.

On 24th April 1924 the northern section from Euston to Moorgate (known as Moorgate Street at that time) was reopened to coincide with the introduction of the flying junctions at Camden Town. The train service was now provided by 'Hampstead' rolling stock. By 1st December 1924 the whole service as far as Clapham Common was being worked by this stock and the special bus service was withdrawn. In consequence, the individuality of the City & South London Railway disappeared, although the name lingered on until the formation of the London Passenger Transport Board in 1933.

Far left Interior of early City & South London locomotive. Note early vertically-placed control handle. The crudity of the equipment is surpassed only by the dangers of injury to the crew!

Left End view of early City & South London locomotive after modification to take additional drawhook for tunnel muck trains.

At the end of the conversion period 50 of the original locomotives, which had totalled 52, were scrapped as they were not suitable for conversion to the four rail system. One of the two remaining, manufactured by Mather and Platt Ltd of Manchester about 1889 but not actually the first, was fitted with the number plates from No. 1 and placed in the Science Museum, South Kensington where it remains to this day. The second preserved locomotive was No. 26, one of a later batch constructed about 1900 by Crompton and Co. This locomotive was retained at Lillie Bridge for a number of years, being exhibited at South Kensington Station between 17th and 22nd December 1928 as part of a display showing progress in tube car design. Subsequently it was placed on a pedestal at Moorgate Station on the Metropolitan Line platform concourse. It was, however, damaged in an air raid in 1940, later being broken up, but certain electrical parts were salvaged and acquired by Crompton-Parkinson Ltd, for their technical museum.

Side view of Loco No. 6, which now has conventional controller with horizontal handle. The air hose at the side was originally provided for charging the air reservoirs for the brakes.

Former Central London Railway locomotive No. 12, which was retained for shunting duties at Wood Lane depot, later known as White City. This loco was one of 28 machines built in 1899 for the opening of the line. It has the modified bogies fitted as a trial in 1901. The loco was scrapped during the second world war.

The third 'tube' railway to be opened in London, the Central London Railway, began working between Shepherd's Bush and the Bank on 30th July 1900. Some lessons had been learned from the two previous installations, the City & South London of 1890 and the Waterloo and City which had been opened on 8th August 1898.

The Waterloo & City had been provided with power cars, one at each end of the train, connected together electrically by means of power cables carried the length of the train along the roof to the cars. This arrangement enabled the driver at the leading end to control both motor cars since at the time of the installation the multiple unit system was not available.

The Board of Trade railway inspecting officers were not prepared to authorise the use of this system for further tube railways because of the risk of serious fusing and consequent fires. The Central London Railway therefore decided to use locomotives but initially suggested that two per train, one at each end should be arranged. While this arrangement would have avoided changing ends at terminals there was still the difficulty of through control even if the main power lines had not been carried down the train, and this would have meant that some form of signalling between the two drivers would have been required which could have been open to misunderstandings. Permission for two locomotives per train, therefore, was not given by the Inspecting Officer and the electric locomotives had to be built large enough and with sufficient tractive effort to handle a complete train, which was envisaged to be of seven car length seating about 350 passengers.

The contract for the whole of the electrical equipment for the railway was placed with the British Thomson-Houston Co, which at that time was associated with the American General Electric Co. The locomotives were designed and built in America being transferred to London in a condition which in modern times would be described as 'completely knocked down'. It is understood that two were completely erected in America and delivered while the others were re-assembled at Wood Lane Depot. These locomotives bore a resemblance to those provided for the Baltimore and Ohio Railroad for the Baltimore tunnel electrification in 1895.

The locomotives were provided with four type GE56A motors which were gearless. The hollow armature shafts were pressed on to the axles with the motor cases constructed round the outside. The bodies of the locomotives were supported on two four-wheeled trucks of the equaliser bar type, of a design approved by the American Master Car Builders Association. The four motors on each locomotive drove spoked and tyred wheels 36 inches in diameter.

The locomotives in modern times would be designated Bo-Bo. They were of heavy construction and described as 'camel back' or steeple cab, being 30 feet long over buffers, with the body itself having an overall length of 26ft 7ins. An unusual feature of the locomotive was that the bonnets on either side of the steeple cabs were divided with a walkway to enable the locomotive crews to enter the passenger cars.

At starting, the four motors were placed in pairs, in parallel, but with each of the pairs in series. A single controller was placed in the centre of the steeple cab

17

Interior of original Central London locomotive, showing power controller which could be operated looking in either direction with the driver standing on the right hand side.

Facing page A pair of Metropolitan District Railway locomotives in Ealing Broadway sidings coupled to one of the special rakes of cars used on the through Southend Expresses.

and used for both directions of running. This large drum, 18ins in diameter, had a control handle almost 2 feet long with a button release for a ratchet to assist the driver to move the control notch by notch. The controller had 22 stages of regulation giving nine series and seven parallel steps, with the remainder used to effect the transition. This long handle for control could be removed and replaced 180° from its original position so that the driver could be in the same relative position for either direction of running.

The provision of gearless type locomotives was arranged because it was thought at the time that geared locomotives in a confined tunnel would be excessively noisy and use additional energy.

The original order placed was for 32 locomotives, but the number actually built was 28 because the section of the railway from Bank to Liverpool Street was not constructed until later, when locomotive haulage had gone out of favour.

The life of most of these locomotives was very short because, unfortunately, soon after operation commenced a serious vibration problem arose. Out of the total locomotive weight of 44 tons, as much as 33 tons was unsprung, mainly because of the heavy weight of the motors, and this caused vibration in adjacent buildings.

Three of the locomotives were converted to take geared motors. These locomotives were provided with new bogies to which were fitted GE55 type traction motors nose suspended within the truck frame. The weight of the locomotive by this means was reduced to 31 tons and the unsprung weight to 11 tons. In addition, experiments were carried out with two 6-car trains converted to the newly developed multiple unit system of motor car control, together with geared motors. This was the first time that the Sprague-General Electric multiple unit system was used in Europe. Trials carried out in 1901 showed that there was a distinct improvement with the geared locomotives, but the problem was almost totally eliminated by the use of the multiple unit motor car trains. A decision was then taken to replace all the locomotives with new motor coaches working on the multiple unit system. The full service was operated by trains working on this principle by 8th June 1903.

The locomotives were offered for sale, but the three geared locomotives were retained for shunting duties at Wood Lane. However, two of these were subsequently sold to the Metropolitan Railway for electric traction regenerative experiments being conducted on their behalf by Mr Raworth. The other geared locomotive (No. 12) was retained to operate on shunting duties in Wood Lane Depot.

Two of the locomotives had been fitted earlier with trolley poles for shunting duties in the depot on sidings which were not provided with the centre third rail but which did have an overhead trolley wire. The passenger rolling stock at this time did not require the provision of a current rail, only the locomotives needed this, so the locomotives provided with trolleys were used to prepare for service the passenger rakes which had been stabled inside the shed roads. Some of the sidings associated with the power house also were provided with overhead wires so that the electric locomotives could be used for shunting coal and other wagons previously serviced by the two steam locomotives numbered 1 and 2 in the fleet. The electric locomotives were numbered 3 to 30.

In 1929 No. 12, which had been retained, was renumbered L21 in the Underground fleet, continuing to be used very spasmodically until the conversion to the four rail system on 4th May 1940, by which time the railway was known just as the Central Line. (This change of name actually took place on 23rd August 1937). The locomotive, the last of the breed, was unfortunately scrapped in 1942 as wartime was not a time when preservation for posterity was given any consideration.

The Great Northern & City Railway, which opened on 13th February 1904, also provided a shunting locomotive at the depot at Drayton Park, which also carried the number 21. The ancestry of this locomotive is obscure but in its final form it bore a striking resemblance to the Westinghouse type locomotive originally operated by the Metropolitan Railway.[1] However, this locomotive had BTH type traction equipment and GE66 traction motors. It was renumbered L33 in the London Transport numbering scheme and was then painted grey.

Efforts were made even under conditions of austerity to save this locomotive as a museum piece but due to several circumstances this was not possible and the locomotive was withdrawn for scrapping on 4th March 1948. This locomotive was never fitted with conventional tripcocks although the Great Northern & City Line was fully equipped with conventional trainstops on 24th November 1935. The vehicle was broken up on site because reconstruction work to accommodate tube stock and resignalling work had necessitated the installation of cable bridges to tube dimensions which made it difficult to move the locomotive between the depot and the main line.

The District Railway, after its electrification, purchased from the Metropolitan Amalgamated Carriage and Wagon Company ten locomotives to enable the through Outer Circle, London and North Western trains from Broad Street to operate over the electrified tracks between Earl's Court and Mansion House. These locomotives were box like vehicles, and usually worked in pairs back to back because most of them were single ended. They began working the Outer Circle trains on 4th December 1905. On the 1st October 1909 the Outer Circle service was cut back to Earl's Court and no longer needed the help of the electric locomotives. They were then used for miscellaneous duties of various kinds but these services did not require the maintenance of ten vehicles and by 1911 three of them had been scrapped.

The locomotives actually resembled the car stock of the period, having the same box like appearance. The body however was shorter with a length of only 25 feet but had the same structure with a clerestory roof. The original ten electric locomotives were numbered by the District Railway 1A to 10A. The seven remaining after 1910 were renumbered L1 to L7.

Negotiations had then been completed with the London, Tilbury and Southend Railway for a through service from Ealing Broadway to Southend. These locomotives working in pairs were allocated for operating the special rakes which were placed on this service, between Barking and Ealing Broadway. The through service to and from Southend began on 1st June 1910 and lasted until 30th September 1939 when it was withdrawn because of the outbreak of the second world war. These electric locomotives were seldom used for any other duty. They were renovated in 1922 when the equipments, including the GE69 traction motors, were replaced by GE260 type, also including the traction motors, which had become available from the reduction of some double-equipped motor cars of 1920 F stock to single equipments. These equipments were restored to the F stock cars when the air door conversion was undertaken on this stock and the locomotives then scrapped.

At the same time as these locomotives were being built, two service locomotives with the same equipment were constructed by the same manufacturer. They were 50 feet long and weighed about 36 tons, but they had controls at both ends. The centre of the vehicle resembled a flat car and was provided with hand operated cranes and winches. The two vehicles were used for hauling ballast, works and breakdown trains as required. They were numbered 21A and 22A.

---

[1] K.R. Benest in his book on Met Electric Locos states that the body of Westinghouse Loco No. 1 was used on this locomotive.

One of the two flat-car type locomotives used for miscellaneous works trains on the District Railway. The two locomotives were built in 1904 by the Metropolitan Carriage & Wagon Company as 'ballast and breakdown motor cars' but were of limited value since they needed current to be switched on to operate. They were scrapped in 1909.

These two service locomotives were withdrawn in 1910 and the vehicles were converted into flat cars while the traction equipment, including the GE69 traction motors, was used on new passenger cars then being delivered. GE69 type traction equipment was in fact ordered from the BTH Co for all District Line rolling stock until the advent of the F Stock. When these two service locomotives were withdrawn they were replaced by the two battery locomotives built by W.R. Renshaw & Co Ltd of Sutton on Trent in 1909.

By 1928 it was necessary to provide a shunting locomotive for the transport of tube cars (in particular) around Acton Works, to enable individual vehicles to be fed into the works and for the making up of trains after overhaul. The progressive system of overhaul in the works required the balancing of the work load by feeding into the works a wide variety of different cars. Two of the Hampstead motor cars then being replaced by new rolling stock were selected for conversion into a works locomotive. The cars concerned were Nos. 1 and 3, built by the American Car and Foundry Company in 1907 for the Hampstead Line. They were cut almost in half, the motor ends placed back to back and spliced together, forming by this means a double ended locomotive. This work was carried out in Acton Works as a special project and completed in 1930. It was the first rebuild of this kind undertaken in the works, becoming a sort of prototype for a number of similar conversions for other purposes undertaken subsequently. This, the first of the Acton Works shunting locomotives, was numbered L10.

The control and motor bogies were virtually unaltered, but some additional equipment was added. The GE69 traction motors originally fitted were retained. They had plain bearings and were without interpoles. The electro-magnetic control equipment was non automatic which was quite satisfactory for shunting purposes.

One of two former battery locomotives built by W. Renshaw for the Metropolitan District Railway in 1909. The batteries were removed during the first world war and the vehicles were converted to mobile stores wagons and renumbered L8 and L9.

Acton shunting locomotive L10 with drawhook fitted to coupler for RCH couplings. It was converted from two Hampstead Line gate stock motor cars in 1930.

The most important additional equipment fitted was an adjustable coupler fitted at each end, which could be raised or lowered to accommodate either tube or surface coupling heights. The couplers were fitted with Ward type heads which at that time were standard on all District and London Electric Railway rolling stock. The only odd coupling to be dealt with at this time was that fitted to Central London cars which had a pin and link arrangement. The coupling at the Ealing end of the locomotive (to distinguish it from the end which actually faced Acton Works known as the Acton end), was rarely if ever used because in Acton Works, being single-ended, all shunting movements feeding the works had to be arranged with the powered vehicle at the Ealing end of the rake. This end of the locomotive in time was therefore cannibalised to provide spares for the Acton end of the locomotive and fell into disuse.

Subsequently the GE69 motors were replaced by GE212 type, which was in fact a very similar motor designed to work with the same traction control equipment, but which had been fitted with interpoles and subsequently with roller bearings. Interpoles or commutating poles, as they were originally called because they were found to improve commutation and reduce flash-overs, were introduced into new motor designs about 1907. GE212 motors were retained for further use from various stock as it was being scrapped because of their superior performance.

Left **L10 in later rebuilt condition and with Ward coupler raised to top position.** Right **Front view of L10 showing the adjustable Ward head coupling and the outline of the plated-over clerestory roof.**

Another locomotive of a similar kind was constructed out of two 1931 Tube Stock Cars, 3080 and 3109, in 1964 virtually to replace L10 and was numbered L11. The two motor car end frames were spliced with plates welded and riveted together. Most of the air piping, the main and auxiliary air reservoirs, together with the brake triple valves and associated piping, were removed from the underframe and placed in the section of the passenger compartment that remained. This made it possible to maintain this equipment without having to place the vehicle over a pit. The four WT54A traction motors were retained, but were connected so that each pair was permanently in series so that they were now working at half voltage, thus providing a better low-speed characteristic for shunting. The normal Ward type coupler at tube stock height was retained at the Ealing end, while at the Acton end two sets of couplers were fitted, each with Ward heads. One was fitted at tube stock height while the other was at surface stock height. This latter coupling could be moved a vertical distance of about 2 inches to enable coupling to be easily achieved with small variations in stock couplings. The tube gear protruded 5 inches beyond the surface gear to facilitate the coupling action of the different types of vehicle. To enable the Ward couplings on the locomotive to match the Wedglock automatic couplers fitted to modern cars, adaptor box couplings were provided. The external communicating door at the Acton end of the vehicle was blocked off and the panel provided with a low level screen through which the driver can see the coupler, to facilitate the coupling action.

Sanding gear was fitted to enable the locomotive to haul a complete 4 car unit up the steep bank towards Acton Town when required. This is fed from a divided hopper in each cab and is fitted with a heater to ensure that the sand is entirely moisture free and therefore flows easily when required. This is now the only tractive unit on London Transport that uses sand. Sand is not now used on the main lines of London Transport at all to avoid interference with the efficient operation of signalling track circuits.

The driver's side cab door at the Acton end has been made like a stable door, so that the driver can look out when performing 'propelling' movements or working in the correct direction but controlled from the rear coupled cab. The vehicle was painted in the miscellaneous vehicles maroon livery, entering service at Acton Works on 19th November 1964, but in 1983 it was repainted in the new Engineers' Vehicle yellow livery.

Acton works shunting locomotive L11 carrying a Ward-to-Wedglock adaptor on the tube stock height coupler with through brake connection. This allowed it to move 1938 and later stocks around the works yard.

In 1906 the Metropolitan Railway acquired 10 electric locomotives built by Metropolitan Amalgamated Railway Carriage Co and with electrical equipment provided by British Westinghouse. They were double bogied camel-back vehicles having four 86M traction motors and were provided for hauling the outer suburban Metropolitan passenger trains within the electrified area. Subsequently, 10 more locomotives were ordered with BTH equipments and while these were also double bogied with four traction motors they were of a box design.

By 1st November 1906 all trains out of Baker Street on the Metropolitan Railway passenger service were electrically hauled, the changeover point to steam traction being carried out at Wembley Park. After Harrow-on-the-Hill Station was reconstructed, the locomotive change was transferred to this location on 19th July 1908. This remained the end of the electrified territory until 5th January 1925, by which time a new fleet of electric locomotives had been provided.

The equipment fitted to the BTH type locomotives proved very satisfactory and in 1913 was removed and fitted to new car stock, being replaced by the less satisfactory Westinghouse equipment which included 86M traction motors. In this way both types of electric locomotive were provided with the same traction equipment. The duties of these locomotives were almost all confined to working passenger trains although occasionally they worked special trains into the tunnel sections to avoid the use of steam locos.

Above **Metropolitan Railway electric locomotive No. 10 outside the Metropolitan Carriage & Wagon works after completion of the body. The electrical equipment has yet to be fitted. The ten locos of this type were equipped by British Westinghouse. They entered service in 1904/5.**

The Metropolitan had a second series of electric locomotives built in 1906 with a box type body and British Thompson-Houston equipment. Seen here is No. 15 in brand new condition.

23

In 1918 an order was placed with Metropolitan Vickers Ltd, Manchester, to replace the 20 existing electric locomotives to improve the power available. It had been intended that the existing locomotives should be modernised and rebuilt but following attention to only two, it was decided to build completely new vehicles. The two locomotives which could be described as rebuilds became Nos. 6 and 17, No. 6 being from the Westinghouse batch and No. 17 from the later BTH batch. The original braking arrangements were insufficient so that the main reason for the provision of entirely new locomotives was to provide stronger underframes to allow improved anchorage for larger brake cylinders. These locomotives were fitted with four MV339 300hp traction motors which were the largest ever used by London Transport and were of similar design to motors used on the Southern Railway. When some of the locomotives were scrapped some MV339 motors were sold to the Southern Region of BR to provide additional spare equipment which was by then difficult to obtain. The Metropolitan electric locomotives were all in operation when the change between steam and electric was moved from Harrow-on-the-Hill to Rickmansworth on 5th January 1925.

No. 15 of the twenty locomotives was exhibited, with one side removed to show the equipment, at the Wembley Empire Exhibition during 1925 and was subsequently named 'Wembley 1924'. The actual decision to name the locomotives was taken in 1927 and No. 17 'Florence Nightingale' was the first locomotive to appear in traffic carrying its nameplates on 3rd October 1927. At the other end of the scale, No. 16 'Oliver Goldsmith' hauled the last regular loco hauled passenger train on 9th September 1961.

No. 5, 'John Hampden' was used for the special train which ran between Baker Street and Aylesbury via Watford on 26th May 1963 as part of the Centenary Celebrations, while No. 1 'John Lyon' repainted, was on duty at Neasden Depot among other rolling stock exhibits. No. 1 was all prepared for preservation but the trucks were found to be cracked and No. 5 was taken in its place and is now on exhibition at the London Transport Museum.

The shunting requirements at Acton Works were assisted for many years by what is now the only remaining serviceable Metropolitan electric locomotive, No. 12 'Sarah Siddons'. This locomotive, used for various duties, is the last active survivor of a fleet of 20 which retained the numbers 1 to 20 throughout their whole period of active duty.

All the locomotives were given names associated with 'Metroland' and although the nameplates were removed during the second world war, names were re-instated in 1953. However, locomotive No. 2, originally 'Oliver Cromwell', became 'Thomas Lord' while five locomotives no longer in active service, No. 9 'John Milton', No. 15 'Wembley 1924', No. 17 'Florence Nightingale', No. 19 'John Wycliffe' and No. 20 'Sir Christopher Wren' were not renamed. No. 9 had been transferred to Ealing Common in 1950 as a shunting locomotive for District Line use. It sometimes operated a stores train to East Ham and was replaced by No. 5 'John Hampden' in 1962. Nos. 15, 17, 19 and 20 suffered early withdrawal after collisions.

Four of the locomotives, Nos. 2, 7, 16 and 18, were sold to BR for experimental purposes. They were taken to Rugby in 1965 but broken up the following year. In addition four locomotives were retained for shunting duties. No. 1 'John Lyon' at Neasden Depot; No. 3 'Sir Ralph Verney' at Ruislip Depot, No. 5 'John Hampden' at Acton Works and No. 12 'Sarah Siddons' at Ealing Common Depot.

The nameplates of all but the retained four locomotives were removed and either sold or presented to interested bodies. One of the 'William Penn' plates was acquired by a Museum at Harrisburg, Pennsylvania, one of the 'Thomas Lord' plates adorns a suitable position at the Cricket Ground while one of the 'Michael Faraday' plates was presented to the Institution of Electrical Engineers but the other remains in the custody of the London Transport Museum at Covent Garden. The 'Sherlock Holmes' plate was taken by the Society which keeps alive the famous name of Conan Doyle's Baker Street detective. Subsequently when 'John Lyon' was withdrawn, the famous boys' school of that name at Harrow-on-the-Hill obtained a plate.

The fate of the last four locomotives has been varied. In April 1965 No. 3 'Sir Ralph Verney' was withdrawn for scrapping after having been used for shunting new 'A' Stock cars about Ruislip Depot following delivery from the carbuilders. After completion of these deliveries there was little work for the locomotive, so it was broken up on site in May 1965 and its remains removed by road vehicles. This locomotive had been transferred originally from Neasden to Ruislip between battery locomotives and to obtain the necessary clearances over this section of the line (which involved at the time reversal at Ealing Broadway and North Acton) the footsteps and shoebeams had been removed.

Facing Page The 20 original Metropolitan electric locomotives were replaced in 1921-23 by new machines of the type shown above. They were built by Metropolitan Vickers. Here No. 14 is passing North Harrow on a Baker Street train in the late 1950s.

In 1970, two 1935 tube stock motor cars were converted to test an articulated design proposed for new rolling stock. The idea was not adopted but the test unit became a works shunter for a time at Acton. Here it is seen during its early testing days.

Moving back to the subject of Tube Stock, on 15th May 1969 two of the 1935 Stock cars, Nos. 10011 and 11011, which had been displaced in 1966 from the Epping-Ongar shuttle by 1962 Tube Stock, were transferred to Acton Works for conversion to a two-car articulated unit for experimental purposes. Consideration was being given at this time to the provision of articulated units for replacing Northern Line rolling stock to avoid the asymmetrical seven-car train formation.

These cars were fitted with three new bogies. The two outer ones were motor bogies of lightweight aluminium construction, while the inner bogie was of steel but of a design enabling articulation of the two carbodies to be achieved. Testing of the unit began in August 1970 and a year later sufficient information concerning the experiment had been obtained. The unit was found to be very useful for shunting duties because of the long shoegear span of over 64 feet, making it very useful for crossing current rail gaps at very low speeds. It was never intended that this unit should enter passenger service and it was transferred to service stock, repainted in the maroon livery and renumbered L14A and L14B. This was in fact the fourth colour scheme these cars had carried. When originally built they had been red and cream and later all red but were repainted 'silver' or aluminium when transferred to operate on the Epping-Ongar shuttle, which was the colour they carried until officially becoming a shunting unit.

In 1975 the lightweight, outer bogies were fitted to 1972 Mark II car 3363 for extended test purposes and the articulated unit cars were broken up at Acton Works in the early part of 1975. However, it had been shown to be useful for shunting purposes and so in 1974, another 'two-car' electric yard locomotive was constructed from redundant 1938 tube stock driving motor cars 10130 and 11130 coupled together. The conversion included the fitting of reciprocating compressors and through power bus-line connections, neither of which were normal on these cars. The vehicles retained the Wedglock automatic couplers at the cab ends. They were renumbered L13A and L13B respectively and were repainted maroon in 1978.

L13A/B, in service stock maroon livery at Acton works, converted from two 1938 stock driving motor cars.

Battery Locomotives

A battery locomotive for all kinds of miscellaneous duties is attractive for an electric railway, since it can be used on non-electrified tracks and when the power supply is discharged on the main running lines. It can draw its power from the normal power supply system when this is available and the recharging of the battery can be carried out during the off peak period.

Hurst Nelson and Co Ltd of Motherwell delivered in August 1905 two battery locomotives for the Underground Electric Railways Company Ltd, for use on the Great Northern, Piccadilly and Brompton Railway during its construction.

The locomotives were 50ft 6ins long over the buffers which were solid central ones as fitted subsequently to the tube passenger cars. The couplers were of the Ward mechanical automatic type then being fitted to the new District Railway electric rolling stock. The overall width of the locomotives was 8 feet. The two locomotives, not unnaturally, were numbered 1B and 2B. They were built throughout of steel with a flooring of jarrah wood planks, on which the batteries rested.

A driver's cab to the full width of the vehicle was provided at each end but at one end a compartment was also provided to house the electrical and braking control equipment. The electrical equipment was supplied by the BTH Company, and was similar to that being provided for the District Railway electrification, including the four GE69 traction motors which were fitted, two to each of the bogies. The vehicles were equipped with hand brakes and a Westinghouse air brake. The GE69 traction motor was a totally enclosed motor without interpoles, having a low continuous rating of about 60hp, but having a one hour rating of 230hp. This was the type of motor not only fitted to the early District Railway motor cars but to the original tube passenger stock as well.

The batteries were located between the two driving cabs, being divided into two sections longitudinally by a lattice girder frame running the entire length of the vehicle. This girder frame formed the ridge support for a series of metal covers over the batteries. There were 80 cells, 40 on each side of the girder, weighing approximately 31 tons and supplied by Chloride Electrical Storage. The total weight of the locomotives in working order was 55 tons.

Each cell had 21 plates and the battery could provide a peak starting current of 800 ampères with a continuous capacity to haul a trailing load of 60 tons at 7mph. These two locomotives were not provided with collector shoes, being used initially on non-electrified track so that recharging and battery maintenance was critical. They performed very useful work in equipping the new Piccadilly Railway, after which they were moved to the Hampstead Railway by road because until 1927 this railway had no physical connection with any other.

One of two battery locomotives obtained in 1905 for equipment supply trains on the Piccadilly and Hampstead lines.

The exposed battery boxes of the Piccadilly battery car 2B. This picture was probably taken during the equipping of the Piccadilly Line and is believed to be at Barons Court.

The success of these locomotives encouraged the Metropolitan District Railway to purchase two similar vehicles but built to District Railway loading gauge. The District locomotives were constructed in 1909 by W.R. Renshaw & Co Ltd of Sutton-on-Trent, and were capable of working off the current rails as well as the battery.

These locomotives were originally numbered 19A and 20A but re-numbered L8 and L9 in 1929 after the batteries had been removed. They were originally used for track maintenance purposes but when Acton Works was constructed in 1922 and work centralisation took place, there became a need for transfer of materials from these new works to Ealing Common Depot, the main running shed for the District Railway. After the batteries were removed, the battery compartment was modified to provide a gondola type vehicle for the carriage of heavy materials. The batteries had actually been removed during the 1914/18 war when the vehicles were mainly used as shunting locomotives at Ealing Common where current rails were always available, so that due to war conditions the batteries were neglected. Replacement of these at the time was not possible because although their construction was similar to those required for submarines, all such production was needed for the war effort.

The locomotives were originally provided with BTH traction control equipment, including the GE69 type traction motors. By 1951 these traction motors had become a maintenance liability and arrangements were made to replace them with the more robust GE212 motors. One of the advantages of the GE212 motor was that it was fitted with interpoles which improved the armature life between repairs. GE69 motors at that time required rewinding on average at less than three-yearly intervals. In 1955 the motors were again changed, this time to the WT54 type, but the original control equipment remained virtually unaltered.

The WT54 type motors provided the advantage that in addition to having interpoles, they were also fitted with roller bearings instead of plain bearings with wool packing, a change which reduced the maintenance requirements further.

Even in 1958 the movement of stores by rail between Acton Works and Ealing Common Depot was still less wasteful of resources than the use of road vehicles, so it was decided that the obsolete traction control equipment of 1909 should be replaced by equipment becoming available from the scrapping of District Railway passenger rolling stock. This equipment, known as the BTH DB260 type, had virtually been the standard since 1923 on all installations until the advent of the 1938 PCM equipment which came with the 1938 Tube Stock. The fitting of the DB260 type equipment ensured that these electric locomotives were fitted with equipment similar in general use to that on the District Q type rolling stock.

These two locomotives became known as the 'Ealing Battery Cars' although they now had no batteries, and did yeoman service until 1969, when a reorganisation of the road lorry fleet indicated that it would be more economical to supply Ealing Common Depot by road in future.

The other locomotive on the Hampstead Line in later life, probably at Golders Green.

When the reconstruction of the City and South London Railway began in 1922 it became necessary to provide some motive power which could be utilised when normal current was not available. Instead of building special vehicles for this purpose, some 'padded cell' trailer cars had their interiors removed and fitted with lead acid batteries and charging resistances. One of the City and South London locomotives was then coupled to each car, the battery being connected to the locomotive at the shoe fuses and the locomotive having the collector shoes removed so that it could not liven up the track. The charging of the batteries could be arranged at certain points in the tunnel by means of special switches with cable connections provided from the normal supply to the current rails. The recharging and maintenance of the battery was of course critical, since the locomotives and battery car had to be manhandled to one of the charging points if the batteries became flat during the progress of the tunnel works.

Much earlier, about 1910, Central London motor car 201 was fitted with a 'Nife' type battery of 370 ampere hour capacity. This car had been one of the four trailer cars converted for trials of the multiple unit control system to try and overcome the vibration problems that had beset the Central London Railway, and which had been used for service vehicle duties subsequently. Originally 200 cells were fitted but in 1932 a further 38 were installed to increase the voltage available.

In 1924 its original running mate, car number 202, also converted to battery operation, was provided with a battery manufactured by Edison Accumulator Ltd, with 30 ampere hour capacity from 263 cells. The batteries were of course placed in what had been the passenger saloon but the first two window bays were replaced by slats or louvres right down to floor level and with louvres inserted in place of windows in other bays. In 1929 these vehicles were given the numbers L22 and L23, which they retained until they were scrapped in 1936 and 1937 respectively. They were known as the Central London battery cars although they worked on other lines on special occasions. They were loaned to the Bakerloo in 1915 for use on the extension then under construction to join this line to the North Western electrification at Queens Park. They were also fitted with outside shoegear to operate on the four rail system so that they could operate satisfactorily on lines other than the Central London Railway, which at that time only used a centre positive rail. This additional shoegear was fitted to the trailer bogie only, there being insufficient clearance available to fit outside shoegear to the motor bogie.

Subsequently two tube 'gate stock' motor cars were converted to operate as battery cars instead of ballast motors. These were two Piccadilly motor cars originally numbered 34 and 39 and built in Hungary. They were subsequently transferred to the Hampstead Line and re-numbered 113 and 118, but in 1936 they were numbered L11 and L12 respectively. They had been provided among a batch arranged for miscellaneous vehicle duties in 1929 on the Hampstead Line following the increased route mileage arising from the extension to Morden and were stationed at Golders Green. These two vehicles were fitted with 220 cells providing 440

L22 and L23 were first used as ballast motors and then as battery cars at White City. The cars — the first multiple unit cars in Europe — were converted from trailer cars as a trial for the Central London multiple unit system. Here the cars have been provided with Ward couplers and fourth-rail shoegear on the trailer bogies for working on other lines.

L11, one of the Hungarian-built tube motor cars, after conversion to battery locomotive.

Interior of battery loco L11.

volts with 280 ampere hour capacity by the DP Battery Company. Subsequently, like the rest of the ballast motors on the Hampstead Line, they interchanged their numbers, L11 becoming L12 and L12 becoming L11 in 1936. This change in the numbering system was brought about mainly from the application of the convention which had been adopted to number the 'A' end vehicles with even numbers and 'B' ended vehicles with odd numbers.

The layout of the connecting loop at King's Cross between the Piccadilly and the Hampstead Line introduced in 1927 meant that cars facing westbound on the Piccadilly became northbound on the Hampstead. For coupling purposes it had become important to recognise instantly the type of car to avoid the necessity of cross coupling the control cables and the brake pipes. Westbound cars were known as 'A' ends and Eastbound cars at that time 'B' ends. In 1938, the 'B' ends became 'D' ends so that the four pairs of wheels on each vehicle could be designated A, B, C and D from the 'A' end to the 'D' end of any car. This system was applied to passenger rolling stock as well throughout the whole of the London Transport railway system.

Another battery car for working on tube lines was completed in 1932. This was Bakerloo Line American Car and Foundry-built motor car No. 66, and was also equipped with DP batteries, a firm which subsequently supplied battery locomotive batteries for many years. With the 6½ ton battery installed, the vehicle weighed 34 tons. The original GE69 type motors remained fitted to the vehicle and it could be operated either directly from the current rails or by means of the battery. When operated from the battery, the motors were connected permanently in series. The DP battery had 220 cells with a 280 ampere hour rating. Additional resistances and manually operated switches were provided for charging the battery. The locomotive was given the number L32 and remained in service until 1948. Although this number seemed out of context the ballast motors had reached the number L29 and the new Hunslet steam engines had already been given the numbers L30 and L31 — in fact the first vehicles to receive this new numbering system in the miscellaneous vehicles series — thus L32 was a logical consequence.

Battery locomotives using the conventional lead acid batteries have one inherent disadvantage, namely that after each period of work on the battery an equal and sometimes a longer period must be devoted to recharging. In spite of this disadvantage, battery locomotives were found to be very useful in maintenance work especially in tube tunnels when it was necessary to discharge the traction current.

A decision was taken in 1936 to place an order for a specially designed battery locomotive rather than a mere conversion of existing rolling stock. The order for nine of these vehicles was placed with the Gloucester Railway Carriage and Wagon Co, although the bogies were provided secondhand, from scrap rolling stock, after overhaul at Acton Works. Three locomotives were provided with metadyne traction equipment which was also secondhand, but the other six had new GEC unit switch equipment.

A metadyne was a rotating machine which changed power at a constant voltage supply to a constant current output. Such a machine is eminently suitable for use with a battery locomotive, except that further deadweight is added to that of the battery which has to be moved in addition to the payload.

The advantages of the metadyne for battery operation, however, were considered sufficient to make an experiment desirable, especially as the equipment used for trial purposes was already available from the metadyne experimental train. Because the metadyne convertor absorbs less power than the equivalent resistances on a more conventional locomotive, the energy consumption was reduced whenever frequent starting was involved. The economical range of speeds, especially at the lower end of the scale, was almost infinite and not dependent on switching of power circuits. This was considered to be particularly valuable for cable laying work, for which a very slow sustained speed was desirable, and originally the metadyne locomotives were utilised on this work. A metadyne locomotive could haul a 100 ton train at a steady 3mph for cable laying for long periods without any overheating of starting resistances.

However, in operation the metadyne control equipment was complex and the maintenance problems of the metadyne machine itself eventually proved unacceptable. Because of this lack of reliability the metadyne equipped battery locomotives were under utilised so that latterly they failed to earn their keep and were withdrawn in July 1977 for scrapping.

The metadyne system was somewhat of a landmark in the development of electric traction because it provided the first successful means of obtaining regenerative braking with a direct current multiple unit traction system.

The metadyne locomotives were numbered L41 to L43 inclusive. The mechanical arrangements and battery construction were identical to the other six locomotives which were provided with GEC unit switch traction control. The metadyne locomotives were provided with the MV145 traction motors which had originally run with this equipment in the converted Metropolitan saloon stock cars which formed the six-car experimental train in 1935.

The GEC unit switch traction control equipment still in use today on the battery locomotives consists of series resistance notching and three motor combinations; all four motors in series; two parallel-series pairs and all four motors in parallel, the connections being made by means of electro-pneumatic unit switches. The grids, which provide the resistance steps, are particularly robust so that the control handle can be held on resistance notches for long periods. There are in fact 28 sequence steps. Arrangements are also made so that at least two battery locomotives can be operated in multiple, either off the current rails or off the battery. In addition, in case of failure, the equipment is arranged to work on the 'half locomotive' principle enabling either motors 1 and 3 or 2 and 4 together with their associated bits of the resistance bank to be cut out.

The locomotives have an overall length of 54ft 4¼ins over coupler faces and a width of 8ft 8¼ins. A cab is provided at each end for the driver. The cab floors, however, are placed at a lower level than the solebars in order to give the operating crews head clearance inside the cab. This factor, however, subsequently proved a source of weakness to the vehicle in heavy shunt or collision conditions.

This is one of three Metadyne-equipped battery locomotives built in 1937 for use on engineers' trains. It is seen at Ealing Common depot as delivered awaiting fitting of its electrical equipment.

A centre gangway connects the two cabs through the switch and battery compartment. The batteries are located on either side of the gangway. There are 160 cells arranged in cases containing 4 cells each. The roof of these Gloucester built locomotives is provided with 24 hinged panels which can be raised to enable the cells to be lifted in and out. In addition, there are 24 detachable louvred panels on the sides of the locomotive which allow access to the body from the side of the vehicle.

The battery provided originally on the 1938 locomotive was of 768 ampere hour capacity, but when these batteries came up for renewal at a later date, they were replaced by a type having 924 ampere hour capacity. The battery life depends on the service it has had to provide and varies from seven to ten years. Improved methods of construction and maintenance will undoubtedly improve even further the life of batteries in the future.

The battery can be charged either when the locomotive is standing on the current rails, or from a shed plug if placed inside a depot. The locomotive picks up current from the live rails by the usual gravity-hung shoes. Arrangements were made in these original locomotives for positive pick-up to be made from the centre rail, with earth return, to enable them to be worked on the Central Line until it was changed over to the LT four rail system on 4th May 1940. These original nine battery locomotives were all fitted with four MV145 traction motors, the type which was in fact used on metadyne equipment being manufactured at the same time. The motors of all nine vehicles were therefore interchangeable, although the metadyne equipped locomotives could not operate in multiple with the GEC type locomotives.

All these locomotives were each fitted with a single compressor which obtained its power from the batteries, not the line, so that they were therefore only wound for a 320 volt supply. The EMB type compressors fitted originally were prone to failure, being particularly susceptible to overheating. In 1953 they were replaced by standard passenger vehicle compressors of the CP30 type, which were then becoming available by the scrapping of the District 'hand worked door' stock, after they had been rewound at Acton Works to work on the lower voltage. This type of compressor was then reclassified CP30D type.

The metadyne locomotives L41-43 weighed some 56 tons in working order, while those with GEC traction equipment had an overall weight of 53.8 tons. The difference was the extra weight of the metadyne equipment. Of the total weight, about 13 tons was accounted for by the battery. The battery locomotives can work at 30mph when supplied by the current rail and at 15mph when the battery supplies the power, hauling a normal average ballast train consisting of about 200 ton trailing load.

In addition to being provided with only one compressor, the original battery locomotives were only fitted with one brake cylinder which was activated by the Westinghouse air brake. This single brake cylinder operated on both bogies through rigging similar to the general Underground rolling stock practice at the time, which only changed to individual brake cylinders for each block on the introduction of the experimental tube stock in 1936. The bogies of the original nine battery locomotives were secondhand motor bogies from Metropolitan Car Stock with 3ft diameter wheels and a 7ft wheelbase. The provision of only one brake cylinder and one compressor made it undesirable for these vehicles to work singly on a train. In the days of steam operation of ballast trains, the single steam engine always ran round the train to make the return journey, the train being routed via crossover points to enable this to be done. However, with battery locomotive powered trains, a locomotive was placed at each end so that running round was rarely required. Subsequently as the use of battery locomotives increased a number of track cross overs all over the system were eliminated. The ballast trains then used the normal passenger train reversing points.

The locomotives were all fitted with three link couplings as well as a tube stock height Ward coupler at each end. Provision had been made for the side buffers to be retracted when the Ward coupling was used. This was done by hinging them back on the upper edge, so that when not required for buffing purposes with main line wagons, they were swung upwards through 180° to rest on concave wooden saddles on the platform over the headstocks.

A solid central buffer was mounted above the Ward coupler. In addition the standard emergency side chains and hooks were fitted for use if a breakaway occurred or if movement had to be made with a vehicle having a damaged coupler.

In 1951 a further seven battery locomotives were placed in service. The main features of the original design were retained. The vehicles, however, were constructed by R.Y. Pickering and Co Ltd, of Wishaw, Scotland, a firm associated with Hurst Nelson & Co but the batteries and traction control equipment came from the previous suppliers. The traction control was almost identical, but the battery now had a capacity of 1008 ampere hours instead of 768.

The traction motors were of the WT54 type made available by the passenger rolling stock replacement programme, suitably modified at Acton Works and designated WT54D type. These motors were reasonably compatible in power output with the MV145 type fitted to the original locomotives.

The principal change in the constructional features of these locomotives, which were numbered L55 to L61, concerned the method of handling the batteries. Runners had been built into the body to carry a small lifting device, which could be positioned to reach any cell, raise it and then move it into a position to be lowered through a trap door in the centre of the vehicle. This enabled the work of changing batteries to be achieved without the use of an overhead crane. A battery locomotive requiring a battery change did not then occupy valuable lifting shop space or occupy the time of the shop overhead crane.

1951 Pickering-built locomotive L56 with a flat wagon and personnel carrier. Note that one buffer is in the stowed position and the other in the lowered position. This was a common sight around depots when shunters used the single buffer instead of both when working full size wagons.

Battery locomotive L76, built at Acton works, shunting a new delivery of 1972 MkI stock cars at Ruislip depot. This loco was renumbered L33 in 1974.

A similar locomotive to those built in Scotland was constructed at Acton Works to test the ability of London Transport's own workshop to compete for this type of work. This extra locomotive to the fleet was provided to enable an overhaul programme to be arranged for the original locomotives. As there had been some pressure to provide additional work at Acton because the reconstruction and modification work on the passenger rolling stock was coming to an end, it was arranged for this locomotive, originally numbered L76, to be built there; it was completed in 1962 and was provided with a 1008 ampere hour battery and WT54D type traction motors similar to the Pickering built locomotives.

At the Centenary celebrations on 23rd May 1963, L76 provided the motive power for the replica of Gladstone's inspection train, propelling this train, headed by Met Rly No. 23, from the rear with four-wheel wagons painted as S & K 29 and S & K 23, the original contractors' wagons on the historic occasion. Battery locomotive L57 also appeared in the official procession at the same celebration to demonstrate the operation of a battery locomotive powered long welded rail train.

When the decision was made to obtain further battery locomotives, the order was placed with Metro-Cammell. Thirteen locomotives were ordered, being numbered L20 to L32. These numbers reverted to an

1965 Metro-Cammell Battery Loco L26 equipped for ATO working on the Victoria Line. The bracket to carry the code sensors can be seen below the step to the side cab door.

33

old series, some of the numbers having been used on earlier battery locomotives. L20, the first of this group, arrived at Ruislip from the carbuilders on 8th December 1964. These locomotives were produced in connection with equipping the Victoria Line and therefore some were fitted with ATO equipment but nevertheless had the replacement of steam locomotives in mind. They were fitted with two compressors to enable them to work reliably as single units, and run round their trains in a similar fashion to a steam locomotive. The bogies, compressors and traction motors were supplied secondhand by Acton Works, the compressor and motors being converted for 320v. GEC provided the control gear, and the batteries came from the DP Battery Co Ltd. The equipment was all similar to that provided in previous locomotives.

While the Victoria Line had been under construction, steam locomotives were still available for miscellaneous work, but after the steam locomotives had been withdrawn and the construction of the Jubilee Line (then known as the Fleet Line) required additional engineering trains, a further five battery locomotives were ordered from Metro-Cammell in 1969. These locomotives were numbered L15 to L19.

As the work load increased, including work on the Heathrow extension as well as the Fleet Line, a further 11 battery locomotives were ordered in 1972, to supplement the existing fleet of 35, and to allow the withdrawal of the three metadyne locomotives. The contract this time however was placed with British Rail Engineering Ltd, for construction of the vehicles at their Doncaster Works. The motors were again secondhand, being obtained from scrapped District Line vehicles, and converted to WT54D type for working down to 320 volts. The GEC traction control equipment was similar to that provided in the earlier vehicles. This batch of locomotives was given the numbers L44 to L54, which then completed the vacant spaces in the numbering scheme except for number L34. In 1954 some of the battery locomotives were provided with electrical sockets to enable a concrete mixer or other power equipment on an adjacent flat wagon to be operated from the locomotive batteries and this facility was provided on the new locomotives.

While the battery locomotives mainly worked in tube tunnels, the limited heating provided in the driver's cab was considered adequate but when battery locomotives were used for the replacement of steam locomotive duties the cab heating provided became unsatisfactory for long trips on cold nights on surface line workings. Improved draught excluders had to be fitted to the cab doors as well as additional heaters in the cabs. These could be switched on before the locomotives were required for duty, to preheat the driving cabs.

The original locomotives, built in 1938, had bogies recovered from the Metropolitan car stock being scrapped at the time. The 1949 locomotives were provided with District Line A type motor bogies, while the Acton built locomotive and the 1965 and 1969 locomotives had Z type motor bogies obtained from pre-1938 Tube Stock motor cars, while the 1973 locomotives had newly built bogies to the Z type design. The secondhand bogies all had white metal axleboxes and suspension bearings, but the traction motors themselves had roller bearings. The new bogies had roller bearings throughout.

Prior to 1962 pneumatic sanding gear was fitted to battery locomotives, but as this equipment was rarely if ever used it was removed and not fitted to subsequent locomotives.

The battery locomotives are provided with a total of four positive collector shoes, one on each side of each bogie, and one negative shoe per bogie In addition, there is a shed receptacle on each side of the locomotive for use in depots. The collector shoes are isolated when the battery is supplying power to the locomotive so that the shoes cannot be made live from the battery. In addition, to prevent the battery locomotive itself bridging a gap in the live rail it was necessary on the earlier locomotives, when working on duties where this might occur, for the shoes to be strapped up out of contact with the current rails. In certain circumstances this was a laborious and difficult job, especially in tube tunnels with limited clearances. A modification was then devised which involved the use of rope cords for easing the work of shoe isolation. One cord was used for lifting each shoe while a second cord was provided to disengage the retaining pawl. Even this arrangement proved to be a tedious and time consuming process but this sort of protection was needed to prevent a section of the railway which would otherwise be 'dead' from being unwittingly livened up by the passage of the locomotives over a gap. A further design modification was arranged which involved the fitting of special circuit breakers to isolate the shoes at the No. 1 end (sometimes called the 'A' end) from those at the No. 2 or 'D' end. This isolation could then be arranged automatically when the locomotive was operating on battery power.

Automatic Train Operation (ATO) was introduced on the Victoria Line from the beginning of operation without conventional wayside signals. This meant that except under engineers' track possessions, battery locomotives working over the line needed to be provided with minimum ATO equipment. The thirteen 1964 Battery Locomotives were therefore equipped with the necessary control circuits for ATO working but only eight of the locomotives (L25-32) were actually provided and fitted with the related control boxes. The additional equipment needed consisted of a small motor generator set to give a 50 volt dc supply for the ATO circuit safety boxes, trip valves and speedometers. The motor generator set was driven from the main battery.

When working on non-coded track (that is basically anywhere other than on the Victoria Line) the operation of the ATO fitted locomotives was the same as for all other battery locomotives having a tripcock in operation. When the tripcock was cut out, an interlock was arranged on the headstock isolating cocks ensuring that the trip valve had to be cut in so that the control of the locomotive was then monitored directly by coded track circuits. When the trip valve was in operation however, the locomotive could still operate on non-coded track circuits but the 'Slow Manual Flag' switch had to be lifted to the exposed position in the driver's cab at the operating end of the locomotive. As long as the locomotive speed was then kept below 10mph, monitored by the mechanical governor energised from the pinion of one of the traction motors, the battery locomotive could move. Otherwise lack of code applied the brakes.

By 1979 there were 43 Battery Locomotives in working order. The three original metadyne equipped locomotives L41-43 had been withdrawn in 1977; L41 and L42 were broken up at Ealing Common, but L43 was retained until 1980 being used for test purposes.

All 43 locomotives are basically of the same mechanical design first introduced in 1938, although they are not all available for every duty. There are two sizes of battery; therefore those locomotives which have more stored power can perform the duties which involve supplying other auxiliary machinery such as cement mixers and drilling machines. Only those locomotives fitted with two compressors can work trains single handed because it has been established that no train should rely upon a single compressor due to the serious problems which would arise from the loss of air due to its failure. Finally, of course, there are those locomotives originally fitted with ATO equipment for working works trains on the Victoria Line but this equipment is now out of use. When works trains run on the Victoria Line it is now done under an engineers' possession of the whole line.

In 1980, two locomotives, L18 and L38, were each modified to carry a drophead buckeye coupling at one end. Up to this time, battery locomotives had had both RCH type drawhooks and side buffers (to enable them to couple to standard main line vehicles) and tube-height Ward couplers, which had in the past been fitted to all tube stock built up to 1934 (except that on the Central London Railway). By 1980, the two types of coupling were fitted to most wagons but the Ward coupler was much lower than the main structural members of the battery locos. This meant that when a heavy shunt occurred while using Ward couplers, there was frequently significant damage from the impact, causing the front end of the loco to drop. These locos were not designed for shunting and have a rather coarsely controlled brake which makes this type of incident more likely. The Ward coupler is now obsolete except on Engineers' vehicles and the buckeye (standard on BR coaching stock) was tried. It provides an automatic coupling in line with the main underframe, thus reducing considerably the likelihood of severe damage during shunting. By pivoting the buckeye head downwards, a standard drawhook is revealed which can be used with a three-link or screw coupling to haul wagons not fitted with buckeyes.

The experiment with L18 and L38 was successful, and slowly since then all locos built from 1964 onwards are being converted to buckeye couplings at both ends. At the same time, retractable buffers (also standard on BR coaching stock) are being fitted to eliminate the heavy lifting required to raise or lower the old, hinged buffers. The combined modification is a considerable task involving replacement of almost the whole end below each cab.

In order to increase reliability & hence availability, a number of other modifications are being done while the locos are in Acton Works. This varies depending on the vintage of the loco, but includes the fitting of new resistor grids, measures to reduce the incidence of flatted wheels and the replacement of some equipment which was secondhand and virtually obsolete when the locos were built. It is expected that this work will enable these locos to continue in service for many years to come but the 14 older ones are not being so extensively renovated due to their limited life expectancy.

A new generation of battery locomotives for miscellaneous duties has been built by Metro-Cammell and delivered in 1985/86, with all the improvements developed in previous battery locomotives having been incorporated, together with some additional provisions. A new departure has been the change from the traditional equipment suppliers, to purchase of the electrical control equipment from Kiepe, which precludes the multiple unit availability with existing battery locomotives. The dimensions of the locomotives have been specified in metric units similar to the contemporary passenger rolling stock since 1969 and are just over 17.7 metres long overall with a maximum weight in running order of about 67 tons. Unlike the previous locomotives, which all had clasp brake rigging operated from one or two brake cylinders, these locomotives have individual brake units incorporating spring applied parking brake arrangements.

In addition to collector shoes and tripcock equipment normally carried on all battery locomotives, sleet brushes have been provided on both positive and negative shoebeams. The collector shoes have been provided with latching up cords with release attachments, which has been standard practice for some years. The power cables are so arranged however that when the traction battery is providing the traction current the collector shoes are isolated, avoiding the cross connection and livening up of the current rails. Shoe latching is now only required when the battery locomotive has to move on and off tracks not provided with current rails and without the benefit of current rail ramps to enable the collector shoes to regain the electrified tracks without damage.

Another innovation with these locomotives is the fitting of buckeye couplers at surface stock coupling height instead of the Ward coupler at tube stock coupling height which was the previous standard for close coupled ballast trains on London Transport. The new hopper wagons and general purpose wagons have been equipped with buckeye couplings and this type of coupling will gradually replace the Ward as standard for this duty. The RCH coupling arrangement has been retained but the retractable buffer is not of the hinged type.

Entry to the driving cab is by a central door in the front of the cab reached by means of a cross walkway and access steps from the track. Appropriate handrails are provided to assist this access arrangement. By this means the level walkway has been maintained completely between the two driving cabs and avoids the dropped cab ends, a feature of all previous battery locomotives, enabling the buffing strength of the locomotive to be increased.

The traction battery provided in the locomotive consists of 256 lead acid cells giving a capacity of 900 ampere hours at the five-hour rate. The battery is divided into two separate sections one containing 160 cells and the other 96 cells. Each section can be selected to provide reduced power either for traction or auxiliary supply. The control power for the locomotive itself is provided by a separate 48 volt battery similar to the type which has been standard on passenger rolling stock. This auxiliary battery provides the control system for the locomotive which employs an earth return, and all the other controls between the locomotive and equipment on trains attached.

The locomotives can operate in multiple by means of control jumpers between the locomotives and arrangements are made so that they do not need to be coupled the right way round for this to be achieved.

A new feature is the arrangement whereby the battery can be re-charged at the same time as motion under traction power is being obtained from the current rails. This facility enables the 'down time' of the locomotive while being recharged to be reduced.

Several sockets for transferring power and control from the locomotive have been provided which will allow both dc and ac power to be available at various voltages for supplying all kinds of equipment external to the locomotive.

The standard communication system, such as Drico and Tunnel Telephone are provided, but in addition a cab to cab telephone arrangement is fitted which can be extended to another similar battery locomotive providing the appropriate auxiliary sockets are connected between the locomotives. In addition, each operator will be equipped with a multi-channel two-way train radio system. By the provision of these facilities the new battery locomotives are versatile and can be used for all purposes.

Another feature not provided on earlier battery locomotives is the fitting of large horizontally sliding cab side windows. These were originally power operated but were modified to hand operation very quickly. The parking brake is spring applied and air released and should there be a loss of air or when the control point is shut down the parking brake is automatically applied. The parking brake may be applied from one cab and released by opening up at the other. The problem of hand brakes had always been that release had to be carried out where application had been made. This was not always accomplished correctly, resulting in seized brakes with consequent operating problems.

To conform to modern passenger rolling stock practice one stabling light is provided in addition to the two headlights and two tail lights provided at each end of the locomotive. Both windscreens of the locomotive at both ends are missile proof and are provided with windscreen wipers. The auxiliary equipment and facilities for the crews of these new locomotives has been developed from the experiences obtained over many years and would appear to be almost the last word in the development of such vehicles.

L65, one of the new design of London Underground battery locomotives. This photo shows it fitted with strain gauge equipment prior to a trial run.

Diesel Locomotives

The 1935/40 New Works Programme of expansion increased considerably the track mileage which was to be maintained by London Transport. Although very little of this was in tube tunnel, a considerable proportion of the additional tracks could only be reached from the London Transport equipment depots at Lillie Bridge and Neasden by passing through tube tunnels. It was therefore not considered desirable to provide additional steam locomotives to service these areas, since it would not be possible to work them for long distances through tube tunnels due to the smoke nuisance, even if they were specially constructed to the restrictive loading gauge. In any event, consideration was already being given to the ultimate phasing out of steam locomotives because the skills required to maintain them, such as those of coppersmiths and boilermakers, were in short supply.

A battery locomotive offered a reasonable solution to the problem, but its availability was a little unsatisfactory because of the time required to recharge and maintain the batteries. Arising out of these problems, in 1936 consideration began to be given to the design of a diesel locomotive which could pass through the tube tunnels. After considerable examination of the problems, work began in 1939 at Acton Works on the construction of a prototype electro-diesel locomotive which could use its diesel engine as the power source when in the open but, due to the noxious fumes and noise produced, work direct from the conductor rails in tube tunnels. Withdrawn Central London motor cars were chosen to form the basis of the locomotive in a similar way to the work already being undertaken to provide Sleet Locomotives.

Two Central London motor cars, Nos. 3937 and 3941, were therefore cut and spliced together back to back with a new central section inserted to form a single locomotive. It was proposed that a fleet of ten of these locomotives would be constructed to replace the steam locomotives, so that a further 18 of the Central London motor cars being displaced were set aside and stored at Cockfosters Depot. The 'Ealing' type motor cars were chosen for this conversion as they were fitted with GE212 traction motors, rather than the older cars with GE66 motors used for the sleet locomotives.

The prototype diesel locomotive was not completed until November 1940 when it was given the number DEL 120. The number was chosen to allow the sleet locomotives being constructed at the same time to be ESL 100 to 119 as there were to have been 20 of these, although only 18 were actually built. The locomotive was originally painted in Metropolitan 'Lake', lined out in gold almost as a steam locomotive of the time, in spite of the fact that there was a war in progress. The paint was, however, available since it was the standard for both steam and electric locomotives at the time.

DEL 120 at Acton works just before being scrapped in 1958. This diesel-electric locomotive was constructed from two Central London 'Ealing Stock' cars and proved to be one of the less-successful Underground designs.

The outbreak of the second world war delayed the expansion of the system and the remaining electro-diesel locomotives were never constructed. Subsequently the efficiency of the 1935 battery locomotives had been considered satisfactory under wartime conditions, while the unreliability of the trial diesel locomotive and its more complicated control system had been a disappointment. The purchase of more battery locomotives was therefore favoured. The opportunity to provide diesel locos was further delayed by the acquisition of the fleet of secondhand steam locomotives from the Western Region of BR.

In the central portion of locomotive DEL 120 a diesel engine was fitted, coupled to a direct current generator. The diesel engine was a six-cylinder, airless injection, two stroke, supplied by Petters. The exhaust was discharged through a large round port placed in the roof. The diesel engine was started by compressed air at 350psi from a reservoir supplied by high pressure cylinders at 1800psi through a reducing valve. When fully charged there was plenty of starting power available for a large number of re-starts.

The electric generator was supplied by Brush and provided an output of 750 amps at 450 volts. The circuitry was so arranged that either the generator or the traction supply would provide the power for the four GE212 traction motors fitted to the bogies. There was a separate traction control equipment for each pair of traction motors so that the locomotive operated virtually as two motor cars in multiple. However when the power was being taken from the generator a system was incorporated which arranged for transition from series to parallel to be delayed on one equipment to reduce the maximum demand from the generator. DEL 120 entered 'revenue' service in 1941 and was the first electro-diesel locomotive to be constructed in Britain. The Southern Region of British Railways subsequently built a number of more powerful locomotives of this kind.

The locomotive first went into service operating the Watford tip train but was often found at Lillie Bridge undergoing repairs since it developed numerous problems, some of which were due to the unfamiliarity of crews with the more complicated controls — a problem often associated with a 'one off' equipment. The metadyne battery locomotives suffered from similar problems.

After the overhaul in 1952, the locomotive was allocated to Hainault where it worked ballast trains for some two years. On a number of occasions when it was not available for duty, the Eastern Region came to the rescue by supplying a steam locomotive. At this time there was still a connection at Leyton for the operation of goods trains, which enabled the substitution to be arranged. DEL 120 was then transferred to Neasden but local residents complained of the noise, especially at night, from the diesel engine.

One of the important jobs performed by DEL 120 was to provide the motive power for a depot works train at Golders Green during the installation of an experimental ground wheel lathe, a duty which necessitated frequently moving in and out of a non electrified road, and after completing these operations it returned to Hainault Depot.

In 1954 the diesel engine was removed and the vehicle operated as an electric locomotive but only on shunting duties and was subsequently allocated to Acton Works. As a shunter required to deal with a miscellaneous collection of vehicles, it was unsatisfactory because the visibility from the driving cabs as well as the access to and from these cabs was difficult and it was seldom used after 1956. In 1958 it was withdrawn and scrapped.

About this time however consideration was again being given to the replacement of the steam engines by diesel locomotives, a practice already well advanced on British Railways. In October 1954 a BR diesel-electric shunter, No. 13018, was borrowed and trials were conducted at Lillie Bridge and Neasden. However this trial was received with little enthusiasm by either the local management or the operators and the problem of the replacement of steam locomotives was again shelved by the acquisition of Western Region steam engines.

At about the same time, consideration was given to the provision of diesel-electric railcars for working the Chesham shuttle service. It was proposed that three of the surplus T Stock motors cars would be converted. Specific proposals were formulated for the work of conversion to be carried out at Acton Works but subsequently it was decided that full electrification to Amersham including the branch to Chesham would be a better proposition and the proposal did not proceed beyond the drawing board.

When BR ceased to overhaul steam locomotives it became obvious that the end of the steam locomotive was in sight and that some steps should be taken to provide a unit for shunting requirements at Lillie Bridge and Neasden, where works trains were normally made up for each night's operation. Battery locomotives as then constructed were unsuitable because they were very vulnerable to damage from rough shunting and because the sighting for the driver was very unsatisfactory, especially in reverse.

To replace the last three steam locomotives which had been retained for shunting duties, three secondhand Sentinel diesel-hydraulic locomotives were purchased in 1971 from Thomas Hill of Rotherham. They had been built in 1967 for use in the open cast iron ore mines at Corby which were now worked out. Each had been provided with a 325hp Rolls-Royce diesel engine built at the Sentinel Shrewsbury works connected by means of an hydraulic drive to the six coupled wheels. These engines were numbered DL81, DL82 and DL83 in order of their arrival on LT premises, but this was in fact the reverse order of their original construction.

It became apparent that the short wheel base of 9ft 8ins of the 0-6-0 wheel arrangement was insufficient for the proper clearance of the signalling system, so that the vehicles were forbidden to move into the track circuited areas beyond the depot precincts. This was totally unsatisfactory at Neasden and very inconvenient at Lillie Bridge. It was therefore decided to provide the locomotives with a tender to increase the overall wheel base. Three K2 bogies — the trailer trucks from the District Line Q Stock then being displaced — were modified which included weighting them to 17 tons and these were permanently coupled, one to each locomotive. This increased the wheelbase to 28ft 6ins. In addition, tripcocks were added to the tender to enable the combined unit to operate as a

Sentinel Diesel locomotive DL83 at Lillie Bridge from the tender end: the tender is fitted with shoebeams to carry the tripcocks. The tenders were required to ensure that the locos operated the track circuits and were mounted on former District bogies.

single vehicle. Although they were always permanently coupled together, the tenders were given separate numbers DT81, DT82 and DT83. The opportunity was also taken to provide sleet brushes on the tenders for the clearance of ice and snow from the current rails so that in addition to shunting duties they could be used for this essential job of current rail sweeping in inclement weather. The livery of the locomotives when delivered was green and this colour was retained even after repainting.

Two locomotives were normally on duty one at each location with one spare to cover maintenance and repairs. Changeovers between Neasden and Lillie Bridge were arranged as necessary.

After the locomotives entered service further problems arose because it was considered that the axle loading at 16 tons was rather too heavy for the short wheelbase, so that the Civil Engineer limited their movements outside the Neasden and Lillie Bridge areas to protect the bridges from overloading damage.

In the early 1980s consideration was again given to replacement of motive power for miscellaneous duties and the controversy concerning the use of diesel engines or providing new battery locomotives was again examined. A British Railways Class 25, No. 25.306, was borrowed for trials but, in the event, new battery locomotives were ordered in 1983.

A 'Unimog' road-rail vehicle coupled to a works train at Neasden. The vehicle shown here is L84. This and another are used as shunters while a third powers a leaf-clearing unit.

BALLAST & PILOT MOTORS

The difference between Ballast and Pilot Motors is small and mainly concerns the work being done. Pilot Motors are used for piloting odd vehicles (perhaps damaged) from one place to another, whereas Ballast Motors are used as motive power for wagons in Engineers' or Ballast trains.

On the tube lines it became necessary from the early days to operate miscellaneous works trains through the tunnels to take in equipment, carry out repairs and to remove accumulated debris and rubbish to avoid manhandling such material and equipment on station stairways. The normal arrangement was to provide the motive power for these works trains by coupling the wagons to passenger motor cars usually arranged back to back, with the wagons in between. Vehicles used for this duty often became permanently engaged on the work and cleaning was neglected so that they never returned to passenger duties, providing sufficient spare passenger stock was available.

These cars could, of course, still be used in multiple by the provision of long hoses and through cables over the vehicles making up the train. It was but a small step to provide the wagons themselves with through cable lines and air pipes.

The Central London Railway converted four of its original passenger cars into multiple unit motor cars for the first tests in Europe of the multiple unit system in 1901. These cars were originally numbered 54, 81, 84 and 88, but after conversion and the provision of motor bogies, together with a switch compartment, they were renumbered 201, 202, 203 and 204 respectively. After the test period was completed, 203 and 204 were converted back to trailer cars, but 201 and 202 remained as motor cars and were then used as the first ballast motors on the Underground system. No. 201 was fitted at one time with tanks, pumps and a perforated loop pipe at the rear platform to enable whitewash to be sprayed on to the tunnel as the original intention of the Central London Railway was that the tunnel would be whitewashed regularly like a farmhouse. Oddly, 201 and 202 were not officially taken off the list of passenger vehicles until 1913. They were converted before World War I to become battery locomotives, and in 1940 were again modified to be able to couple to the so-called Standard Tube Stock (later known as the Pre-1938 Tube Stock) by the fitting of a Ward type coupler in place of the pin and bar.

When it was decided to relay the Central London track, these vehicles were used to haul some special long wagons called 'dreadnoughts' to take the new track into the tunnel. These wagons, which were specially constructed, made it possible to carry 42 foot lengths of track already made up complete with sleepers, into the tunnel to the working sites from Wood Lane Depot. This type of train was the forerunner of the modern long-welded-rail trains.

Following the end of the first world war some service improvements were necessary in the passenger facilities on the tube lines. Forty new cars — 20 trailers and 20 control trailers — were built by Cammell Laird of Nottingham, delivery being completed by August 1921. These cars, the 1920 stock, were the first tube stock to be equipped with air-operated doors, but could not be used in service until some existing motor cars had been converted to run with them. Twenty of the original motor cars for the Piccadilly Line were selected for conversion by the Gloucester Carriage and Wagon Co, but this work was not in fact completed until 1923. The first two motor cars however, were converted by Cammell Laird as early as November 1920. The period of conversion was extended because all the cars could not be released at one time.

Central London Railway motor car No. 201 as a ballast motor car. This was one of four trailer cars which were converted to motor cars in 1901 to test the multiple unit system. It subsequently became a battery locomotive and was numbered L22 by the Underground.

Originally a French built gate stock motor car No. 7 for the Great Northern, Piccadilly & Brompton Railway, this car was converted to air doors by the Gloucester Carriage & Wagon Company in 1921 and renumbered 483 in 1926. In the conversion a doorway with a single leaf was installed. Several of the cars were subsequently converted to ballast motor cars, when this doorway was generally resealed. The number L26 was allocated in 1936.

In 1930 these 1920 stock trailer cars were modified to run with new motor cars after which they were placed on the Bakerloo Line, but the motor cars originally converted to run with them were then withdrawn from passenger service. Twelve (486-496 and 499) were scrapped, but six (480, 482, 483, 484, 485, and 497) were converted at Acton Works for use as ballast motor cars, remaining on this service until 1952. They were renumbered L24, L26, L27, L28, L29 and L25 respectively in the 1930 renumbering scheme. In 1936 they were again renumbered to make the vehicles conform to the convention which had by then been established that 'A' end cars should have even numbers and 'B' end cars odd numbers. They were in fact renumbered in pairs, the original L24 becoming L25 and the original L25 becoming L24. L26 and L27 were dealt with similarly and so were L28 and L29.

The remaining two cars in this fleet (481 and 498) were converted into double-ended passenger cars for working the Aldwych shuttle service. Part of the renovation work included the fitting of GE212 motors with interpoles instead of the original GE69 type not so provided. These two cars each had four numbers in their life span. After construction in Hungary, they were numbered 5 and 30 in the original Piccadilly fleet, but after conversion to air door operation, in the 1926 renumbering scheme they became 481 and 498. In 1929, after modification for the Aldwych service they were renumbered 186 and 185. Subsequently, in the final 1936 London Transport renumbering scheme they became 3282 and 3283 respectively.

The Aldwych shuttle service was operated by these two cars from February 1926 until the second world war, the service being withdrawn on 21st September

French built Piccadilly car No. 10 was renumbered 484 after conversion to air door operation to work with 1920 Cammell Laird stock and was one of two motor cars converted by Cammell Laird for this purpose. The single leaf sliding door was opened over a recessed panel with a window. When converted to ballast train duty in 1930 the vehicle was renumbered L28, but it became L29 in 1936.

Two of the Piccadilly motor cars converted to air doors in 1920-21 were again converted to double-ended cars for use on the Aldwych branch in 1930. In 1948 they became full time ballast cars. No. 3282 is seen here at Northfields depot at one end of a ballast train.

1940. When it re-opened on 1st July 1946, these two cars were again used to provide the service for a short time. However, during the war years they had been used for a number of purposes, including service as the Cockfosters-based shelter refreshment train.

The two cars 3282 and 3283 were withdrawn from the Aldwych working in December 1949 when they were used as pilot motors for the transfer of rolling stock to and from Acton Works and between depots. For a short time they were coupled on either side of a flat wagon and used as a Northfields depot stores train from Acton Works. This arrangement did not entirely eliminate the use of road lorries to and from Northfields Depot, and was found to be less convenient. Another duty undertaken by 3282 and 3283 was the operation of the infrequent stores train to Queens Park and Croxley Green Depots on the Bakerloo Line.

The main purpose of this stores train was to transfer brake blocks, oil and cleaning materials for use at these depots. The operation was never more frequent than once a month and sometimes the stores movement was at even longer intervals. Queens Park Depot was not accessible by road and Croxley Green Depot was also laid out to receive material by rail rather than by road. When special vehicles for this service were not available, an ordinary passenger train was used. The two cars were last operated on this duty in January 1956 and were afterwards withdrawn for scrapping, which took place in December 1956. They were never given miscellaneous vehicle numbers but carried their passenger stock numbers to the end.

After the bombing of London began in 1940, sustenance was provided to the nightly shelterers in tube stations by the running on all the lines of trains with refreshments. The train operated from Cockfosters on the Piccadilly Line was worked by motor cars 3282 and 3283 on some occasions. On other lines, passenger units were usually diverted for the purpose. The refreshment trains were first introduced in November 1940 on the Central Line, then on the Piccadilly and Northern Lines and finally in December on the Bakerloo Line. There were in fact six trains operating, provided with 50 food containers which were loaded for each nightly run.

The service provided on the Bakerloo Line was unusual because the train did not operate from a depot but from a siding at Willesden within the jurisdiction of the main line railway. This train operated from here as far as Piccadilly Circus and back until July 1941 when it was withdrawn. The supplies to the stations used for sheltering on this line were then delivered by road.

The trains on the other lines ceased operating in 1942 when the bombing of London eased and the shelterers no longer used the tube stations. However, with the start of the bombing by the so-called 'doodle bugs', or pilotless planes, the shelterers returned and the service was restarted in December 1943 on the Piccadilly Line, the train running between Cockfosters and Hammersmith. Then in February 1944 the service on the Central was restarted, the train running from Wood Lane to Liverpool Street and back. The next month saw two more trains re-introduced on the Northern Line, one running from Morden Depot to Euston on the city side while the other ran from Golders Green to Kennington by way of Charing Cross and then back to Finchley Central, returning to Euston on the city side before going back to Golders Green Depot. By May 1945 all these services had been withdrawn.

Gate Stock ballast motor car L16 stored at Acton works awaiting restoration for preservation. Subsequently this vehicle was scrapped in 1960 as the cost of renovation was unacceptable, but the gate end was retained and restored by the apprentices at Acton works as a training exercise. It is now at Covent Garden Museum. L16 was originally Hungarian built motor No. 51 for the Piccadilly Line.

Even before all the 'gate' stock had been withdrawn from passenger service, a number were converted for ballast train working and miscellaneous duties, being renumbered in the 'locomotive' fleet list to follow on from the Acton shunting locomotive L10. The first two were therefore numbered L11 and L12, having been originally Piccadilly Line Hungarian-built motors cars with the fleet numbers 34 and 39 respectively. These were converted into battery locomotives for operation on the Hampstead Line during its reconstruction which involved considerable work at Camden Town, Charing Cross and subsequently at Kennington. In addition, four others renumbered L13, L14, L15 and L16 became ballast motor cars. L16 was scrapped at Ruislip in 1960, after being stored since 1955 with a view to restoration and preservation. In the event, because of the deterioration of the vehicle and the expense involved, it was decided that the most prudent thing was to preserve the gate end of the car only, since this was the part that was completely different from what followed in rolling stock design. The end was cut and restored by craftsmen and apprentices at Acton Works, and is now part of the London Transport Museum collection. All the four vehicles were ex-Piccadilly motor cars originally numbered, 42, 41, 44 and 51 respectively, but did not have batteries fitted. They usually worked in pairs and were of course single ended.

The Hampstead Line reconstruction work begun in 1922 involved the provision of flying junctions at Camden Town to enable Hampstead trains to run over the City and South London Railway without interference with the original Hampstead Line service. At this time the Hampstead Line had no physical connection with any other railway and the equipping works trains had to be loaded and unloaded at Golders Green. Although new passenger rolling stock was on order for the line, considerable additional rolling stock was required as well for the extension to Edgware from Golders Green and for the operation of the City and South London section when it was joined on. Hampstead trains began working to Moorgate on 20th April 1924 and through to Clapham Common on 1st December 1924. It was not until 31st January 1929 however that the last 'gate' stock ran on the Hampstead Line, which was the first tube line to cease using this type of stock. Other lines had to help out with providing vehicles for the miscellaneous duties required for the extensions and new works.

The Piccadilly Line seems to have had surplus stock and further Hungarian built motor cars from that line, numbered 50, 53, 71 and 57, were taken for miscellaneous duties, being renumbered L17, L18, L19 and L20 respectively. It is not now clear how these particular cars were selected, but there had been some considerable stock movements between the Piccadilly, Bakerloo and Hampstead Lines as the last two lines needed additional stock while the Piccadilly had a surplus. Until the extension of the Bakerloo to Queens Park and beyond, all these transfers had to be made by road.

The Hampstead Line was not connected into the network until the loop connection at King's Cross with the Piccadilly was opened on 27th March 1927. Following this connection, ballast motor cars became easily interchangeable from line to line, although there were still a number allocated particularly to each line. Subsequently control of the miscellaneous vehicle allocation was centred on Lillie Bridge.

L75, originally 577, built in 1923 for the Hampstead Line and renumbered 3517 in 1935, was converted to a ballast motor car in 1954. This was one of the few cars almost totally enclosed when reconstructed for this duty. It lasted until 1978.

In 1930 some additional ballast motor operations were required to assist in the work being undertaken to extend the Piccadilly Line to Cockfosters and the four tracking of the line between Hammersmith and Northfields, so three more pairs of passenger motor cars were converted for this purpose. Authority for the conversion was obtained in 1930 and the vehicles chosen were those already mentioned that had been converted to air door operation.

In 1934 there were 14 ballast motor cars, numbered L13-L20 and L24-L29, to which must be added five battery locomotives, L11, L12, L22, L23 and L32. By 1953 it was possible to release 14 of the oldest pre-1938 tube stock from the Central Line for conversion as ballast motor cars to enable the earlier vehicles, which were becoming extremely difficult to maintain, to be scrapped. The replacements were all selected from 1923 tube stock and were converted at Acton Works. All were available for ballast duty by early 1955 and were renumbered L62-L75.

Several of these vehicles were actually converted into ballast motors because they happened to be already at Acton Works undergoing repairs after damage in collisions. No. 3500 for example was one of the vehicles involved in the serious collision at Stratford on 8th April 1953 which involved fatalities and serious injury of passengers. Nos. 3452 and 3463 were damaged in shunting collisions at Acton and Ruislip respectively in 1952. These cars became L64, L62 and L63 respectively.

When first converted these vehicles were painted grey, but in 1957 it had been decided that miscellaneous motive power vehicles should be painted in Metropolitan maroon. This decision was assisted by the fact that the paint store at Acton Works still had a quantity of this paint available and by this time only a small fleet of vehicles were required to be painted in this colour.

In 1963 L72 sustained collision damage and as Pre-1938 Tube Stock was then being scrapped in large numbers due to the introduction of the 1959/62 Tube Stock it was decided not to carry out repairs, but convert another car instead. No. 3376, a 1927 Metro type car, was selected for conversion and renumbered L72 — the same number as the damaged one, which was then broken up at Acton Works. Later, on 16th March 1967, L73 was badly damaged at Golders Green in another shunting mishap and a further vehicle was required as a replacement. This time 3183, a 1931 Metro type car was chosen, becoming available for miscellaneous vehicle duty in May 1967. However, on this occasion the vehicle did not take the same number as the vehicle it replaced and was renumbered L77.

By the end of 1977 most of the Pre-1938 Tube Stock type of Ballast motors had been withdrawn. L63 and L68 were used for leaf clearing duties late in 1977 which was their last official duty. The complete fleet had been disposed of by September 1978. L68, L74, L75 and L77 were scrapped at Ealing Common, L65 at Ruislip and L63, L64 and L71 at Neasden.

Ballast motor cars are mainly provided to meet the civil engineering requirement for works trains for numerous purposes concerned with the installation and maintenance of the track and of equipment associated with the operation of the railway including at times bridge renewals. However it is also necessary to move rolling stock not in train formation from depot to depot and between depots and Acton Works, often as 'dead' cars, and 'pilot' motor cars are required for this purpose. When these special moves were very intermittent it was the practice to use passenger motor cars for the purpose. When unit stock was introduced however, single motor cars were not capable of operating on their own since the necessary equipment was spread over the unit and it became the practice to provide special pilot motors to move vehicles as required.

Until the pre-1938 Tube Stock cars were withdrawn, passenger motor cars of that type were usually used for this work, but after the introduction of the 1959 Tube Stock, transfers of individual cars and parts of units between lines became commonplace and eight Pre-1938 Tube Stock cars were specially set aside to act as permanent pilot motors in addition to the ballast motor fleet. These were a mixed collection of 1927 and 1934 Stock motor cars.

Subsequently they were used to augment the ballast motor fleet from time to time and in February 1967 it was decided that they should be painted maroon and numbered in the ballast fleet. The actual numbers of the vehicles were as follows (with the L numbers subsequently allocated shown in parentheses):— 3690 (L130), 3338 (L132), 3370 (L134) and 3380 (L136) were the A end cars, and 3693 (L131), 3707 (L133), 3701 (L135) and 3273 (L137) the D ends.

In the event 3338, 3707, 3380 and 3273 were not renumbered, being withdrawn by 1971 without the repainting or renumbering having been carried out.

Two 1934 stock motor cars Nos. L130 and L131 (formerly 3690 and 3693) were converted to Pilot Cars in 1967. They are seen here at Acton works in December 1982 following their repainting in the new standard yellow livery for service vehicles.

No. 3273 however received a new lease of life being transferred to the Isle of Wight as S15S in March 1971 to replace one of the original cars of this type operating there which had been damaged. The Pre-1938 Tube Stock for operation on the Isle of Wight, 43 cars in all, was modified at Acton Works between 1964 and 1966 and despatched to the island in small batches so that the electric services between Ryde Pier and Shanklin could begin on 20th March 1967.

The other four cars earmarked for the miscellaneous fleet, L130 (3680) together with L131 (3683) and L134 (3370) together with L135 (3701), working as pairs, were retained for pilot duties and survive to the present day.

It was also necessary in the rolling stock replacement programmes to provide pilot motors for the transfer of surface stock cars. With the reformation of all District Line trains into seven-car trains commencing 4th October 1971, the withdrawal of District Stock from East London Line service in 1974 and the scrapping of the surplus cars, such pilot motors were in considerable demand to enable transfers to Ruislip Depot to be made where the final disposal and scrapping was arranged.

In 1967 Nos. 4198 (Q23) and 4211 (Q27) were utilised for this duty as well as providing the motive power required for the surface line gauging car. In 1971, however, four of the Q38 type motor cars, 4416-4419 inclusive, were specially selected for pilot motor duty. In March 1972 these motor cars were renumbered L126, L127, L128 and L129 respectively but were not repainted in miscellaneous vehicle livery until several years later. On 10th October 1972, L127 had an extraordinary mishap running unmanned down the Ealing Common Depot incline towards Acton Town station. A serious accident was prevented by the sand drag at the bottom of the incline, placed there for the purpose of safeguarding against just such an eventuality. L128 and L129 were withdrawn in January 1983 for scrapping but L126 and L127 remain available for use.

In addition, from 1970, six surface line driving motor cars were retained for shunting scrap cars and new deliveries of surface stock at Ruislip Depot. These were 4204 (Q23) and 4323 (Q27), 4264 (Q23) and 4319 (Q27) and Q38 cars 4409 and 4420. All were scrapped in 1972 except the Q38s, which lasted until 1974. They were never renumbered as pilot cars.

Q38 type pilot motors L126 and L127, converted in 1972 from a batch of 25 driving motors obtained for Q Stock for the District Line in 1938. These were cars 4416 and 4417 respectively. They were painted yellow in 1983.

45

Ballast motors L146 and L147, ex-1938 tube stock motor cars 10034 and 11034. The marker light has been replaced with twin headlights close together with a stabling light below. The tail-light arrangement has been left unaltered but the Wedglock coupler has been replaced by a Ward coupler and train and main line hosepipe connections raised to the waist-rail level. A bracket for the high-level headlight for ballast train working is also fitted.

1960 tube stock pilot motor car L133 (ex-3905) at Ruislip depot immediately after delivery from BREL's Derby carriage works on 1st May 1987. This together with its partner L132 (ex-3901) will haul TRC666 (see page 77) around the system every three months.

When new stock for the District Line began to arrive in 1977 at Ruislip Depot, Pilot Cars were required to shunt it and the resultant scrap stock around the depot. Initially, two pairs of CO/CP stock were retained for this duty: 53247-54053 and 53001-54193. The C77 stock being delivered at the time was commissioned at Ruislip and made its way to Hammersmith Depot under its own power for use on the Hammersmith & City, Circle and Edgware Road to Wimbledon services. When the D78 stock was delivered to Ruislip Depot from 1979, it was already largely commissioned, the final work being done at Ealing Common Depot. Consequently, there was not only a need to move scrap stock from Ealing to Ruislip, but also a need to provide motive power for each new unit's journey to Ealing, and this was provided by more pilot units of CO/CP stock. All these pilot cars were stencilled at each end of each side with notices indicating that they were not for scrap, to avoid them being included for the time being in the scrapping programme. The first 2 pairs of pilot cars to be provided for the transfer work were 53003-54003 and 53262-54211 but were followed in 1980 by 53210-54210, 53223-54035 and 53028-013063-54235. One unit of new or scrap stock was transferred at a time, between two pilot units. When scrapping of the R stock got under way, three 2-car units of it were designated pilot units for the same purpose. These were 22624-23544, 22629-23519 and 22661-23561. All of these pilot cars were eventually sent for scrap except 22624, 53028 and 013063 which have been privately preserved.

When 1938 Tube Stock became available for scrapping by the introduction of the 1972 Tube Stock, it was decided to convert a number of these driving motor cars into ballast cars. This conversion was more difficult in some ways than that previously undertaken, which had required only bodywork modification. 1938 tube stock driving motor cars required the fitting of compressors, the removal of the Wedglock couplers and the fitting of Ward type couplers together with alterations to the air pipe hose couplings.

The conversion work began in Acton Works in 1972 when four cars were dealt with. These were 10088 (originally L84 but subsequently renumbered L140) and 10021 (L142) as A ends, and 11067 (L141) and 11065 (L143) as D ends.

In later stages, 10257 and 11027 became L144 and L145 respectively in 1975, 10034 and 11034 became L146 and L147 in 1976 and 10022 and 11104 became L148 and L149 in 1977. 10327 and 11327, which became L150 and L151, were particularly interesting because they had previously been driving motor cars of the odd nine-car train stock and had therefore already been modified several times in their lives. The modifications included one previous numbering change, as they had started life as 90327 and 91327 respectively.

46

When the last series of these cars was undergoing conversion at Acton Works it was decided that one pair should be adapted to act as a weed killing unit when required, by equipping them with hoppers and appropriate dispensers to avoid providing special vehicles just for this purpose. The vehicles chosen for this were L150 and L151. Two cars specially arranged for weed killing duties had been provided in 1935 for the District Line, being kept at Ealing Common depot. They had been obtained by modifying a motor car and a control trailer car of what at that time was called the Local Stock, which was formed from what was left of the original 1905 B Stock of the MDR. The motor car was numbered 8 and the control trailer 1712 in this fleet. They were equipped with tanks and spray nozzles which were fed by gravity to spread the weed killing fluid. The cars were renumbered WK840 and WK841 respectively.

However it was found that the single motor equipment provided insufficient power, so the control trailer was replaced by another 1905 motor car which was renumbered WK842 in 1937. The control trailer was subsequently scrapped.

The two weed killing cars were used intermittently but the war caused the requirement to be neglected and the vehicles fell into disuse. The cars were scrapped in 1950.

Further 1938 tube stock motor cars converted in 1978 to ballast motors were 10266 and 11266, becoming L152 and L153, and 10141 and 11141 which became L154 and L155.

By 1979 there was a total requirement for 16 ballast motor cars for various intermittent duties. In some cases it had been the practice to make up some Works Trains with a battery locomotive at one end and a ballast motor at the other with separate crews dependent on whistle signals if any joint working on the run was required. Usually the battery locomotive provided the main motive power on these trains while the ballast motor was called upon to perform a small portion of the work at the working site providing the traction supply was available. In addition, it provided accommodation for the transportation of the personnel.

It was normally the practice to work the ballast motors in pairs but this confined their working to times and routes where traction current was available. The normal duties of ballast motors included the provision of motive power for at least two rubbish trains, composed of two or three flat wagons carrying waste containers, which ran around the system at specific times, usually after traffic hours, collecting station rubbish and other debris. Other miscellaneous duties include powering trains from the permanent way depots at Ruislip, Neasden, Northfields and Lillie Bridge, including weed killing and moving stores and specialised wagons to working sites, relieving the more powerful and versatile battery locomotives for more important duties. One advantage that the ballast motors possess is the ability to provide accommodation for personnel and small tools in the body of the vehicle, which is impossible with battery locomotives.

Weed-killer train at work. Several former District Railway motor cars of B stock were converted to weed-killing cars in 1930 and lasted until 1950.

WORKS & MISCELLANEOUS VEHICLES

10-ton wagons

The original 'maids of all work' were 10-ton ballast wagons, and this type of vehicle has been used for general duties since the construction of the first underground railway in 1863. A large number of 10-ton open wagons were owned by the Metropolitan Railway and a smaller number by the District Railway, but as more specialised wagons for specific duties were obtained the 10-ton ballast wagons became rather the exception in the make up of works trains, and are not now used at all.

One of the duties where old 10-ton open wagons ended their days was to service the Power Station at Neasden, in the form of ash and slurry wagons. During the time the station was coal fired there was a large amount of debris to be removed for disposal. The wagons allocated to ash and slurry duties were not allowed to leave Neasden Yard and received very little maintenance because they were virtually mobile storage bins until the refuse they contained could be removed for dumping elsewhere. Ash and boiler debris was a useful material for filling and drainage on construction sites, but the demand was never continuous so that it had to be stored until required. Subsequently, on the conversion to oil firing at the station, the number of wagons wanted for these duties was reduced and the wagons became known generally as Power House wagons, of which there were 16 when Neasden Power Station closed. The numbers of these wagons were prefixed by the letters PH for Power House, A for Ash or SL for Slurry Wagon. Power house debris which arose at Lots Road and Greenwich Power Stations was removed either by road or Thames barge directly, so that railway wagons as such were not required.

Some of these 10-ton ballast wagons had a very long life — even as late as 1980 there were two on the books which had been originally constructed before 1900. These, BW4 and BW214, both of 1897 vintage, were transferred to the Bluebell Railway and the LT Museum respectively in 1982.

Metropolitan 10-ton wagon No. 71, built by Cravens in 1891 and transferred to the LNER in 1937. It was typical of the many low-sided wagons taken over by London Transport and retained for use in engineers' trains.

Flat wagon BD704, seen here carrying a breakdown emergency bogie, was built by Ashbury in 1897 for the Metropolitan Railway, who used it at Neasden power station.

F329, a small flat wagon of 10-ton capacity, being used as a tank wagon. It was one of a batch obtained in 1935.

The centenary celebrations at Neasden in 1963. The replica wagons, specially adapted from 10-ton ballast wagons, are occupied by LT staff dressed up to depict Mr Gladstone's party inspecting the first section of the Metropolitan opened.

49

A flat wagon on the City & South London Railway converted from one of the passenger cars and carrying hand-operated winching devices. It was used in connection with the reconstruction of the line in 1921/22.

City and South London Railway reconstruction
The first major work of reconstruction undertaken on London's Underground was the enlargement of the original City and South London Railway tunnels from a minimum of 10ft 2ins to at least 11ft 8¾ins, to allow for the passage of Standard Tube Stock and so that the Charing Cross, Euston and Hampstead Railway could be joined to it to become one railway, later known as the Northern Line. The actual work began in 1922 and was partially completed by 20th April 1924 when trains from the Hampstead Line began working south as far as Moorgate. For the tunnel work, 22 flat wagons were constructed from old City and South London Railway cars which were no longer required. These wagons were made up into what became known as 'muck trains' for removing the spoil and debris arising from enlarging the tunnels. The trains themselves were brought to the surface at Stockwell Depot by means of the depot lift. Six to eight of these flat cars could be hauled by the electric locomotives when power was available, but in addition two of the locomotives were semi-permanently attached to old passenger cars which had been adapted to house lead acid batteries for supplying power to the locomotives when current was not available.

It had been intended that the work of enlarging the tunnels would be carried out without shutting down the train service completely, but the section between Euston and Moorgate, because it was virtually paralleled by the Metropolitan Railway, was closed from 9th August 1922.

A subsidence occurred at Newington Causeway between the Borough and Elephant and Castle on 27th November 1923 which, in retrospect, might have been disastrous. This accident caused a re-appraisal and the railway was then shut down for passenger operation while the work of enlarging the tunnel proceeded. Prior to this accident a passenger service had been maintained from 6.30am to 7.40pm between Moorgate and Clapham Common.

Couplings
The railways of the Underground have always had specialised couplings and several different types have been used. Even on a single line there have been couplings that were incompatible. The Central London Railway originally had a link and pin type for the passenger rolling stock which remained in operation until the London Transport four-rail system was brought into use on the Central Line in 1940, at which time the Ward coupling became standard.

The arrangement of centre drawhook with a three link chain attached, together with the provision of side buffers at main line railway height was for many years known as the RCH coupling. It was standard throughout Britain for loose-coupled wagons, which were exchanged between railways under the control of the Railway Clearing House.

When the District Railway was electrified in 1905, the Ward coupler was adopted for coupling mechanically all its passenger stock. It was subsequently used as the standard coupling on the tube railways associated with the District at that time — the Piccadilly, the Bakerloo and the Hampstead (now part of the Northern). The coupling on tube stock, however, was at a lower height than that on the District vehicles. It was possible to make a coupling between vehicles at the two heights without the use of match wagons by fitting a special 'swan-necked' Ward coupler bar to one of the cars concerned.

The Ward coupler takes its name from the Rolling Stock Engineer imported from America at the turn of the century as part of the engineering team brought over by Yerkes to electrify the District Railway. F.D. Ward patented his automatic coupling device and received royalties for several years even after he returned to America in 1905. The Ward coupler was adopted by the Underground Group as the close coupling arrangement for ballast and works trains with the coupling at tube height to allow the use of tube stock motor cars for hauling wagons.

The Metropolitan Railway adopted a form of 'buckeye' coupler for use with most of the electric passenger stock from the beginning of electrification, retaining the RCH close coupled screw link type coupling for steam passenger and freight working, but this arrangement was not developed by London Transport. A form of buckeye has however become standard on all British Rail's loco-hauled passenger stock and some multiple units.

With the standardisation on unit-type passenger rolling stock in 1938 and the introduction of fully automatic 'Wedglock' couplers to couple units together, the general use of the Ward coupler has progressively reduced and has become costly to provide solely for ballast train working. The Ward coupler, having outlived its usefulness, is now being gradually replaced on locomotives and wagons by the standard British Rail style of drophead buckeye coupler at the 'RCH' height. Although older wagons have tube height Ward couplers, almost all of them also have the RCH hook and chain coupling as well. If one of these needs to couple to a buckeye-fitted wagon, it is achieved by dropping down the buckeye head to reveal an RCH type hook to which a three-link or screw coupler can be attached.

Match Wagons

The match wagon is another type of wagon used for special intermittent duty and over the years there has been a relatively large fleet of such wagons owned by London Transport. Match wagons are used to enable vehicles with incompatible couplings to be made up in the same train. They are placed between the two vehicles with dissimilar couplings and have the appropriate couplings at each end.

With the extension of the Central London Railway to Ealing Broadway on 3rd August 1920, where a physical connection was established with the District Railway, and the opening of Acton Works in 1922, Central London cars were transferred to Acton Works for overhaul and required match wagons for the journey. They could not get there under their own power due to the three-rail system of the Central London Railway and had to be hauled. These Central Line match wagons had link and pin couplings at one end and Railway Clearing House (RCH) ones for coupling to a steam locomotive at the other. The use of match wagons is now largely confined to the transport of new or scrap vehicles when hauled by locomotives over British Rail's metals. Movement on the Underground of a train of vehicles with incompatible coupling arrangements is usually achieved by the use of coupling adaptors which are fitted and removed at each end of the specific journey undertaken.

Match wagons are usually required in pairs and such pairs are normally kept together when not in use. Those owned by London Transport were often converted from 10-ton ballast wagons with whatever type of coupling was required. They usually had to be loaded with scrap iron or ballast to provide satisfactory stability. For a number of years the fleet consisted of four surface type match wagons and eight tube type converted from ballast wagons. The problems of maintaining in serviceable condition these old wagons which were only needed intermittently, usually when a new rolling stock programme was under way, made it often necessary to limit their availability to within London Transport railways only or severely restrict their operation over British Railways.

Some match wagons were used on special duties. MW537 for example was allocated for use as a stores wagon for Drayton Park Depot where only very light material could be delivered by road. Access to the depot was by way of the main line goods yard at Finsbury Park. This wagon was scrapped in 1969 and transfer of stock between the Northern Line (Highgate Wood) and Drayton Park ceased on 1st October 1970.

The car builders usually delivered new cars between match wagons provided either by themselves or the main line railways and it was also usual for scrap cars to be taken away similarly between match wagons owned or hired by the scrap merchant.

The advent of the 1935/40 New Works Programme involved the delivery of a large number of new cars and the consequent scrapping of some old ones. At this time the new cars were delivered from car builders at Gloucester or Birmingham to Lillie Bridge by the appropriate main line railways between match wagons, and sometimes there were problems getting these wagons back in time for the next delivery. LT match wagons were then normally used to transfer the new tube cars composed of 1938 Tube Stock to Ealing Common and on to Golders Green where they were prepared for service.

In order to maintain this extensive programme of vehicle transfer, twenty-six 10-ton ballast wagons originally from the Metropolitan Railway fleet were converted to match wagons of various kinds and some of these lasted on this sort of duty for many years, the last pair being scrapped in 1978. Subsequently after the war a further six 10-ton ballast wagons were converted but none of these were kept in service beyond 1978. Nowadays, match wagons required are provided by the conversion of brake vans.

A 10-ton former Met Railway wagon of 1896 vintage converted to match wagon MW531 with RCH coupling at one end and a Ward at tube height at the other. The wagon is branded 'piped only' which means it carries a through brake pipe but is not itself Westinghouse braked.

Brake Vans

In the days when all the motive power was provided by steam locomotives, one of the important components of a works train was the brake van. Works trains were usually provided with two brake vans, one at each end, so that to reverse direction, only the steam locomotive had to run round the train and additional shunting to get the brake van at the rear was unnecessary. The provision of the leading brake van was also useful for conveying personnel to the working site.

The original brake vans used by the Metropolitan and District Railways were of 10-ton capacity but subsequently 20-ton brake vans were obtained.

London Transport numbered the original District Railway brake vans B195 to B200. Ex-Metropolitan Railway brake vans of 10-ton capacity transferred for ballast workings were numbered B561 to B575. These were in better working condition, having been maintained as part of the Metropolitan Railway's freight train fleet and allowed the scrapping of all but three of the District vehicles by 1936. In 1935, London Transport obtained from Hurst Nelson, six 20-ton brake vans for use on works trains. These were numbered B555 to B560 and allowed three of the Metropolitan vans to be scrapped before carrying their new numbers. This accounts for the gaps of B568, B570 and B571 in the numbering scheme.

Twenty-five brake vans of various types had been acquired by London Transport when the Metropolitan fleet was absorbed on 30th June 1933. Most of these were subsequently taken over by the London & North Eastern Railway when steam traffic operation, including the goods working, was transferred to that main line railway. On 1st November 1937, 186 low sided wagons, 44 covered goods wagons, 15 cattle trucks, four bolster wagons, three machinery wagons, four 10-ton brake vans and nine 20-ton brake vans were transferred to the L&NER as part of this deal.

Other brake vans in the fleet had been renumbered B550 to B554 and were an odd collection. The oldest District Railway van dating from 1890 was a lightweight of only nine tons and was numbered B550. This vehicle was withdrawn and scrapped in 1940.

Two ex-Metropolitan Railway ballast brake vans also dating from 1890 were numbered B551 and B552. One of these, B551, was scrapped in 1950, but B552 was branded "CME return to Ealing Common" and lasted until 1969. B553 and B554 were 13-ton brake vans dating from 1914 and were also ex-Metropolitan Railway stock and withdrawn in 1969. (B561, a 10-ton brake van scrapped in 1962 was also branded for CME use only and used for transfers to and from Acton Works and Ealing Common.)

Consideration was given in 1959 to the replacement of the old Metropolitan brake vans since they were then becoming a maintenance liability, and a British Railways brake van No. B954309 was hired to see whether such vehicles would be suitable for use on London Transport. This van was fitted with roller axle bearings which at the time were considered unsuitable for intermittent ballast train duty with long spells of idleness, so another van E300276 was obtained, in September 1959, fitted instead with plain axle bearings. It is considered unsatisfactory to hold roller bearings supporting heavy weights in one position for long periods because it has been found that this results in the pitting of the races and early failure of the bearings. Plain white metal axle bearings on the other hand were renewed at regular periods but in fact always remained in the same weight-supporting position whether moving or idle. Brake vans on ballast train duty often stood for very long periods without movement.

The chimney for the stove in the guards accommodation of the BR van had to be reduced by three inches to clear the LT loading gauge. Negotiations were then begun to obtain seven surplus vans of this type from British Railways, but this proved difficult at the time and instead an order for six new vans was added to the British Railways manufacturing order placed at Ashford works, for supply to London Transport. The six vans were then given the numbers B580 to B585, becoming operational in February 1962. The gap in the continuity of the numbering system arose because B576 and B577 had been given to Metropolitan passenger coach brake vans which were in fact very little used, B576 being scrapped in 1939. One distinctive feature of LT brake vans was that the Metropolitan Railway practice was followed of painting the ends of the vehicles red.

In 1949 two special brake vans were constructed to run with the diesel electric locomotive DEL120. Two of the 10-ton four-wheeled flat wagons constructed in 1936, F330 and F327, were fitted with a sentry box type structure made of steel and glass to tube loading gauge. The vehicles were also fitted with a hand brake and an emergency Westinghouse brake handle so that the ballast guard could apply the brake if necessary when the train was running fully braked. After conversion these brake vans were numbered within the brake van series but with the prefix F so that these numbers became FB578 and FB579. They were not withdrawn when the diesel locomotive ceased working, being used on stores trains hauled by a single battery locomotive to such depots as London Road and Queens Park on the Bakerloo Line and East Ham on the District, which were depots without easy road access and, with the exception of East Ham, could not be approached by steam engine. Subsequently they were converted to operate with the long welded rail train when hauled by steam locomotives.

With the withdrawal of steam engines from active service, the role of the brake van diminished and, while a number were kept for special duties, most were scrapped. B558 was painted in a special maroon and yellow livery for working as a brake test instrumentation van with Metropolitan electric locomotive No. 12 'Sarah Siddons', and was on exhibition at the London Transport Golden Jubilee exhibition at Neasden on 24th April 1983. Four of the BR built batch were taken to W.H. Davis and Son of Langwith Junction near Mansfield, to be converted to match wagons. B583 and B584 were converted in November 1980 to become surface stock match wagons to cover the work involved with the removal of stock to the scrap dealers subsequent to the introduction of D stock on the District Line. These wagons also received the numbers LTE95800 and LTE95801 respectively so that they could be recognised by the BR 'TOPS' computer system whilst travelling over BR metals. B580 and B585 were converted by W.H. Davis and Son in early 1983 to tube stock match wagons for use in the disposal of 1938 Tube Stock.

Former District Railway passenger brake coach converted for use in ballast trains. It may also have been used as a tool van.

One of six brake vans constructed in 1935 by Hurst Nelson for ballast train working. Some of these brake vans of 20 tons are still in use for miscellaneous duties.

The special brake vans FB578 and FB579 converted in 1950 from 10-ton flat wagons. They were specially adapted for use in long rail trains.

Personnel Carriers

When works trains were made up with two brake vans, the carriage of personnel to the site was achieved by utilising the one that was not required by the train guard. The interior of ballast motors — the old passenger accommodation — could also be used similarly but no such space was available when battery locomotives were used. The difficulties of getting personnel to the working site had to be overcome to enable battery locomotives to perform the duties of the steam locomotives. The practice then developed of including a ballast motor in the train make up to provide the accommodation for personnel and not as a motive power unit. When the 1962 Tube Stock was delivered, which replaced most of the old pre-1938 Tube Stock, some of the trailer cars were retained from the scrapping programme to become Personnel Carriers.

Six 1931 vintage ex-Piccadilly Line trailer cars were selected and converted at Acton Works for this purpose during 1965/66 and they were re-numbered PC850 to PC855. The upholstered seating was removed, the interiors were fitted with wooden seats and the outsides painted in the miscellaneous vehicle colour scheme of maroon. Birmingham built cars 7061, 7063 and 7080 became PC850 to PC852 respectively, 7158 (a Gloucester built car) became PC854 and 7071 (another Birmingham car) became PC855. PC853, renumbered from 7114 and built by Birmingham, was damaged in 1970 and was not repaired. No. 70518, a 1927 built Metropolitan Carriage trailer, was converted to replace it and renumbered PC856. This car had originally been numbered 7518 but, along with 57 other trailers, had been modified to run with 1938 Tube Stock in 1938 when it was given the number 70518. These 58 cars originally only had two pairs of double doors down each side with no end doors, unlike the 1931 stock used for personnel carriers, but this car, 70518, along with another similar car had been modified in 1957 to provide end single passenger doors similar to the 1931 Stock.

Subsequently problems arose with these personnel carriers under winter conditions because they were not provided with heaters. Arrangements were therefore made to fit a number of them with a form of storage heater which could be pre-heated from collector shoes fitted to shoebeams carried on one of the bogies. A trailer bogie from a Pre-1938 Tube Stock motor car had to be selected for these cars, so that the appropriate shoebeams could be fitted.

In 1979 it was decided to allocate four 1938 Tube Stock cars for personnel carrier duties and motor cars 10165, 10182, 11150 and 11165 were set aside for this purpose, to be converted as and when manpower and facilities at Acton Works were available. Non-driving motor cars were originally selected for conversion but driving motors were chosen because it was considered desirable to have a handbrake available and this was already fitted, whereas if trailer cars or non-driving motor cars had been chosen, this equipment would have to have been fitted additionally. In fact, only three were done, 10165 and 11165 of those already mentioned and 11247; these were numbered PC859/858/857 respectively.

Personnel carrier PC855, converted from Pre-1938 tube stock trailer car 7071 built by the Birmingham Railway Carriage & Wagon Company for the Piccadilly in 1931. The long hosepipe on the compressor line is provided to allow cross-coupling to match to similar vehicle ends A to A or D to D. The narrow hose is the compressor line and the broad hose the brake pipe. The shoe gear has been provided to incorporate a car heater inside the vehicle for winter working.

Personnel carrier PC858 converted in 1980 from 1938 tube stock motor car 11165. The shoegear provides the feed to the interior storage heating equipment.

Flat Wagons

The vehicle that has taken over the role of 'maid of all work' from the four-wheeled, 10-ton open wagon is the ubiquitous bogie flat wagon. These have been built and used since the earliest days of the twentieth century and the oldest vehicle of this type inherited by London Transport was an ex-Central London Railway vehicle of 15 tons capacity, built in 1900. Numbered 1 in the CLR fleet, it became F125 under the LER and started the flat wagon series in 1936 renumbering scheme as F300. This vehicle was withdrawn and scrapped in 1968.

The flat wagons originally owned by the LER for tube line use had Ward couplings and centre buffing gear only, while a number used solely by the District were arranged to have similar couplings at District Railway height. These early vehicles had a capacity of only 15 or 25 tons and the last to survive still exists as a jib carrier for a diesel-electric crane.

The Underground fleet of flat wagons owned by the District and the London Electric Railways when combined were numbered from F100 upwards starting with six vehicles obtained from Metro-Cammell in 1931. Originally numbered F1 to F6 by the District Railway, they became F100 to F105 and in the 1936 renumbering scheme they became F310 to F315.

The standard flat wagon since 1931 has been the 30-ton vehicle just over 50ft in overall length. Vehicles of this type were fitted with through main line and train line pipes and Westinghouse brakes, with a handbrake operated by hand wheel on each bogie. They had Ward couplers at tube stock height to enable coupling to ballast motors, and drawgear and hinged buffers to enable coupling to steam or battery locomotives with RCH couplings as an alternative. The buffers on the superstructure were hinged back when the Ward coupler was used.

Flat wagons have been used for a wide variety of duties, especially where passage through or work in tube tunnels is necessary. They can be fitted with water tanks for damping down the track to reduce dust in dry conditions, or with pumping equipment and sludge tanks to get rid of excess water and mud in other circumstances. Other flat wagons have been fitted with timber fenders between which were placed containers to provide refuse collection through the tube tunnels. Flat wagons are in fact generally adaptable to carry a great variety of things such as cable drums, compressors, cement mixers and general stores and sometimes, after adaption for a particular duty, they retained the equipment required for long periods, being moved about the system as needed.

The fleet of 30-ton bogie flat wagons began to be acquired in 1931 when the six wagons were obtained on the District Railway account from Metro-Cammell and numbered F1 to F6. Three of these wagons still survive but only one, F315 (F6), is available for general use as a flat wagon. F311 (F2) was fitted with water tanks to provide supplies for concrete making and other such duties at locations remote from water supplies and was later modified to provide the water supply for the leaf clearing train for use in the autumn (see last chapter).

London Electric Railway 15-ton flat wagon originally numbered F115 and built in 1907 for operation over tube lines. It was provided only with Ward coupling and no buffing gear. The wagon was renumbered F303 and converted during the second world war as a stores wagon, being used to transfer material and parts between Acton works and Northfields to save lorry mileage. As fuel became less scarce this arrangement ceased and the wagon was then used for store movements to and from Queens Park and Croxley. The central enclosed section was subsequently removed and the wagon remained in stock until 1980.

In 1935, eleven 30-ton flat wagons were obtained from Gloucester Carriage and Wagon Co. These wagons were originally numbered F89 to F99 and were subsequently renumbered F316 to F326 but not respectively. In addition, there were four 10-ton four-wheeled flat wagons from the same builders. These were numbered originally F85 to F88 but subsequently renumbered F327 to F330. Of these latter wagons, F327 and F330 were later converted to the special brake vans FB579 and F578 respectively.

A number of these 30-ton wagons are also still operating, F316 being fitted with a compressor, but most have been withdrawn and scrapped.

A further ten 30-ton bogie flat wagons were obtained form Gloucester in 1937 for the work involved in the 1935/40 New Works Programme. These were numbered F331 to F340, and some of these have subsequently been refurbished while others have been scrapped because they had become beyond economic repair.

F331 and F332 have become permanent tank wagons while F336 was reconditioned in Acton Works purely as a flat wagon in 1981. F340 has been converted to a concrete breaking wagon, having had a powered hammer on a beam mounted on it.

A further thirty-one 30-ton flat wagons were obtained, again from Gloucester, in 1951 and these were numbered from F341 to F371. Some of these wagons during 1982/4 were re-conditioned by W.H. Davis. F342, F343, F345, F350, F351 and F355 were converted to concrete mixer wagons, and F344, F353, F357, F358, F365, F366 and F369 were refurbished including the fitting of buckeye couplings and retractable, rather than hinged, buffers at both ends. F341 had been fitted with tanks for gully emptying in connection with the operation of a pump train. F347 along with F388 and F397 from a later batch of 30-ton flat wagons, were provided with turntables for the laying of small cables for signalling, telephones and other control systems.

F352 was provided with equipment for trench digging and F356 was adapted for carrying bins for what was described as the 'muck' train.

Some occasionally had even more mundane duties. F314 of the 1931 batch was used as a storage wagon for battery locomotive traction batteries, during the time the locomotives were under heavy repair, while F362 provided mobile accommodation for the historic Metropolitan Jubilee coach body which is awaiting restoration as a Museum exhibit.

A further four wagons of the type were obtained from Gloucester in 1956, numbered F372 to F375, while in 1958 two, F376 and F377, were constructed in Acton Works. In 1959 Gloucester supplied a further six, numbered F378 to F383. Of these only F380 was earmarked for special duties having a compressor fitted for servicing pneumatic tools.

In 1964 new wagons for the miscellaneous fleet were ordered from BR workshops. The order consisted of fifteen 30 ton bogie flat wagons, F384-F398, twelve 20 ton bogie rail wagons and three 10-ton four-wheeled flat wagons. All the bogie wagons were built at the BR workshops at Ashford, Kent, while the four-wheeled wagons were constructed at Shildon in County Durham. A number of the flat wagons have subsequently been reconditioned by W.H. Davis & Sons, being fitted with buckeye couplings and retractable buffers. In addition, F395 was fitted with prototype bogies for test purposes.

Forty-one further wagons were delivered in 1984/5 from Procor, the successors of Charles Roberts. These have been designated general purpose wagons and have been allocated the numbers GP901 to GP941. They are fitted with buckeye couplings, retractable buffers and through control and brake lines. These wagons, which do not have Ward couplers, will cover the duties previously provided by flat cars and ballast wagons, and will allow an equivalent number of old wagons to be scrapped.

30-ton flat wagon F341 converted as a sump wagon for drainage clearing work. F341 was one of thirty-one 30-ton flat wagons constructed in 1951 by the Gloucester Carriage & Wagon Company. It is seen here at Ealing Common depot.

The special rake of cable wagons used for laying heavy power cables. The wagons are close-coupled but the outer ends have both Ward and RCH couplings together with folding-back side buffers.

A number of flat wagons were reconditioned by W H Davis & Sons, some being fitted with concrete mixers and power sockets. F350, a wagon originally built by the Gloucester Carriage & Wagon Company in 1951, is seen after being so equipped.

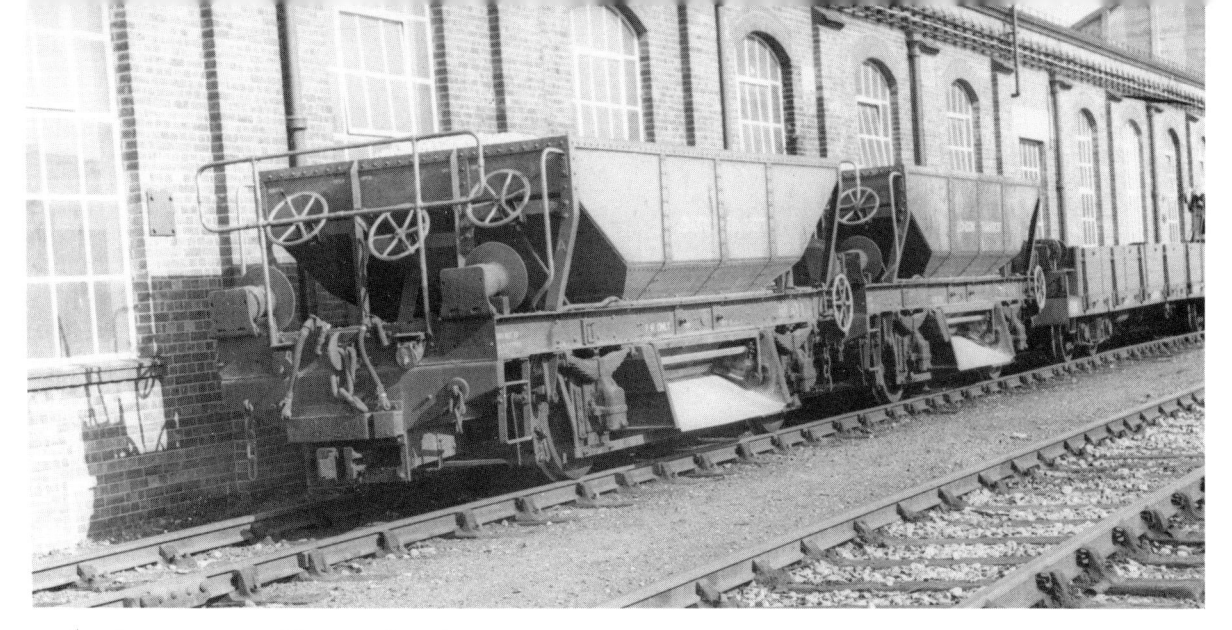

Two hopper wagons of the two-axle variety, which began to be withdrawn in 1981. They had Ward couplings and RCH drawgear with retractable buffers. The wagon nearest the camera, HW433, was acquired by the Bluebell Railway in 1982 for retention as a working relic.

Hopper Wagons

Over the years, the practice developed of providing specialist wagons rather than relying totally on the ubiquitous 10-ton open wagon or, later, the 30-ton flat wagon. One of the best known is the hopper wagon and in 1935 London Transport obtained seven four-wheeled vehicles of this type, each with a capacity of 20 tons. Their benefit was in the way that ballast could be unloaded at the site by special chutes fitted to the wagons, thus avoiding the hand shovelling which was required when 10-ton open wagons were used. They were built by the Gloucester Carriage and Wagon Company and were originally numbered HE230 to HE236 but were renumbered HW400 to HW406 in the 1936 renumbering scheme.

A further five vehicles were purchased in 1938, these being built to assist in the new track laying programme required for the 1935/40 New Works Programme. In 1951 a third batch of hopper wagons, also from Gloucester, brought the total up to number HW434. Finally, three more 20-ton hopper wagons were obtained from British Railways in 1965 bringing the number up to HW437.

These four-wheeled hopper wagons were prone to derail at some awkward locations due to their long wheelbase. As a result, BR refused to accept them over certain routes for the conveyance of the fresh limestone direct from the quarries and this refusal limited their usefulness. Some 20,000 tons of limestone ballast for the railway tracks of London's Underground are required to be moved about the system annually from Neasden, Lillie Bridge and Ruislip Depots and sometimes other depots on the system, to various sites according to requirements.

In recent years, these wagons have been withdrawn from service and disposed of, but not all have been scrapped. They have been an attractive proposition for a number of the many preserved railways around the country. HW402 and HW433 were transferred to the Bluebell Railway, HW421 to the Colne Valley Railway, HW426 and HW429 to the North Norfolk Railway and HW435 and HW437 to the Isle of Wight Railway. HW410, 411 and 436 were part of a batch sold to W.H. Davis & Son but were later resold to the Severn Valley Railway and two of these were included in the steam-hauled freight train at Newport in September 1985 as part of the Great Western 150th anniversary celebrations.

In April 1980, tenders were received for the supply of thirty-four 30-ton bogie hopper wagons to replace the older ones. The new wagons, of which 22 were built, were provided from the beginning with retractable buffers and buckeye couplings instead of the Ward or RCH type and this began the new era for ballast trains working on London Transport. The wagons were provided with through control lines so that they could be arranged in rakes with two motive power units, one at either end, but controlled in multiple from the leading vehicle.

One of the new bogie hopper wagons was exhibited at the Private Wagon Federations Exhibition at Olympia in March 1981, when it had the number HW438. This was based on the assumption that the new wagons were going to follow on the existing hopper wagon numbering system, but in the event a new set of numbers was established, the new vehicles entering service as HW201 to HW222. The vehicles were built by W.H. Davis and Son, of Langwith Junction in 1981.

The provision of bogie wagons for general miscellaneous duties, although more expensive initially than four-wheeled wagons, stems from the search for cheaper track maintenance. Four-wheeled wagons require the provision of check rails at many curves to prevent derailments, and to be held to speed restrictions which are difficult to enforce or which are unacceptable if the ballast train is required to work between passenger trains.

The withdrawal of the four-wheeled wagons will enable the number of places where check rails are provided to be reduced without the imposition of speed restrictions.

The Instruction Train

During the second world war it became necessary to provide some training for semi-skilled staff who were required to ensure that trains operationally complete were satisfactory and safe for passenger service. Such staff were not required to have the mechanical skill to repair in detail any particular piece of equipment, but were required to establish that it was functioning properly. Staff normally employed in this work had previously picked up their skill in the hard school of experience but as equipment became more complicated, proper training was necessary. After the end of the war consideration was given to the provision of a mobile training school which could travel round the depots providing training as required.

Some old tube rolling stock which had been withdrawn from service just before the war but which had been stored, was selected to provide an Instruction Train. Five cars from the fleet of 1920 Cammell Laird stock, which had been the first stock with air operated doors to be provided for tube line working, were the vehicles taken for conversion. The cars were subsequently numbered IC1075 to IC1079 inclusive and finished in a special amber and black livery.

Each instruction car contained specialised training equipment for demonstration and operation by the trainees. IC1075 had previously been control trailer 5170 when stored, the only one of the five cars which had been a control trailer. It was equipped with Metro-Vick pneumatic type traction control equipment, a bench containing Wedglock couplers which could be coupled and uncoupled, a motor generator set with its associated control equipment, and a demonstration of the different car lighting circuits, especially those still powered from the 600 volt traction supply.

IC1076 had been trailer car 7243 when stored and was converted to provide a small lecture room and an office for the instruction staff. The lecture room could hold 12 students comfortably for sedentary instruction from a blackboard or slide projection.

IC1077 had been trailer car 7248 and was converted to demonstrate the various types of Westinghouse brake equipment in use as well as containing an air compressor to provide the appropriate compressed air for this equipment.

The interior of one of the five cars of 1920 tube stock built by Cammell Laird for the Piccadilly Line after its conversion to Instruction Train. It was used to train rolling stock maintenance staff between 1949 and the late-sixties.

IC1078 had been trailer car 7241 and was provided with all the different types of door control and door gear, including replica door mechanisms then in use.

IC1079 had been trailer car 7235 and had a complete PCM type traction control equipment mounted on a frame to simulate the conditions on the underframe of the modern type of rolling stock. (A similar arrangement has since been provided for demonstration purposes at the London Transport Museum at Covent Garden and can be operated by the visitors to the Museum.) In addition, on this car the conventional electro-magnetic contactor type equipment used on the older stock was installed for demonstration.

The conversion of these cars was carried out at Hammersmith Depot as and when equipment became available. Detailed mechanical work on the equipment was carried out at Acton Works but the cars themselves did not pass through the works. Installation was completed in 1949, after which rolling stock staff training began. The five cars were incapable of movement on their own, having no propelling equipment, but were transferred between depots by pilot motors or ballast motors when necessary. It was proposed, however, to keep a pair of CLR motor cars to operate with this train, 3977 and 3988 being reserved and kept for this purpose. However, this did not materialise and the two cars were scrapped in 1949.

At the Centenary Celebrations on 23rd May 1963 the train was put on exhibition as well as taking part in the rolling stock parade. On this occasion it was formed into a train with ballast motors L66 and L71.

An Operating Department training school which included demonstration equipment had been opened at Lambeth North station by the Underground Group on 4th February 1920. This training school was located above the station itself and therefore was reasonably accessible from most parts of the system at that time. It was enlarged in 1948 but the 1935/40 New Works programme had included plans for larger premises to cover the enormous expansion of the system then envisaged. It was not however until 22nd October 1963 that a brand new training centre was officially opened at White City on the site of a Central London Railway car shed — part of what had been known as Wood Lane Depot. The premises at White City were actually brought into use on 23rd September 1963 and the Lambeth North accommodation was then made available for other purposes.

Initially it had been thought that there was still a need for the Instruction Train as well as the new Training Centre at White City because the staff being trained had different functions and conditions of service. It soon became apparent however, that the training requirements were complementary, often needing the same equipment for demonstration, and eventually the Instruction Train was spending most of its time at White City on the track alongside the new Training Centre. As the older equipment was phased out of service it was obvious that the new equipment should not be duplicated in a training train and it was later arranged that the training arrangements would be combined and the equipment installed in the Training Centre. The Training Train, which had been of immense value in the immediate post-war years, was scrapped in May 1969.

TRAVELLING CRANES

Most engineering works of a major character on the London Underground system are carried out by contractors who generally supply their own equipment as needed, including cranes. However when the working site was specifically part of an operating railway and it was necessary to locate the cranes required on the railway lines, London Transport and its predecessors owned and provided the cranes required. In addition goods yards and working depots required some form of cranage from time to time and cranes were often required to serve these locations.

In spite of this, the story of travelling cranes and their associated jib carriers is difficult to produce as a continuous one since the information available tends to be contained in isolated incidents. A crane is often required for a specific job and then subsequently goes into obscurity until the next time it is required at an entirely different location for an entirely different job.

Curiously enough the vehicle which began the numbering series for cranes, introduced by London Transport in 1936 with C600, was a hand-operated crane constructed by Jessop & Appleby in 1895, being one of two cranes numbered C180 and C181 in the earlier Underground numbering system.

Another hand-operated crane which eventually came into the possession of London Transport was the 5-ton Cowan and Sheldon crane built in 1914 which was owned by the Metropolitan and Great Central Joint Committee and used mainly in the Harrow-on-the-Hill Goods Yard but also in the Northwood Goods Yard if required. The crane was the only item of rolling stock owned directly by the Joint Committee because all the services over the joint lines set up by an Act of Parliament in 1905 were provided by the two constituent companies, originally the Metropolitan Railway and the Great Central Railway and subsequently London Transport and the London and North Eastern Railway.

The crane was No. 1 in the ownership of the Joint Committee but was renumbered C619 when taken over by London Transport on the 1st January 1948 after nationalisation. Although the crane was withdrawn from active service in the Goods Yard in 1955, it still exists because it was acquired for use by the Quainton Railway Society — a preservation society at a location which was once within the territory of the Joint Committee. The goods yard at Harrow ceased to function in April 1967.

District hand-operated 10-ton jib crane mounted on a six-wheeled frame. This was probably C180, which was scrapped in 1935.

District Railway five-ton mobile hand-operated crane on a four-wheeled frame. This Jessop & Appleby crane was numbered C181 in the Underground series and C600 by London Transport. Its principal use was at Ealing Common and Lillie Bridge depots but spent a period at Aldenham bus overhaul works before being scrapped in 1953.

Two travelling cranes which were disposed of by London Transport soon after its formation in 1933 were one from the Central London Railway, working at Wood Lane Depot, and another from the City and South London Railway, originally working at Stockwell Depot. These had been renumbered C185 and C186 in the Underground system. C185 was a 5-ton crane with a four-wheeled 6ft wheelbase originaly obtained in 1900 and had just been renumbered C601 in the London Transport scheme when it was scrapped in May 1937. C186 was never renumbered by London Transport.

The District Railway possessed two 5-ton Grafton four-wheeled steam cranes which became C182 and C183 in the fleet numbering system. C182, which had the maker's number 828 and was obtained in 1905, operated at a steam pressure of about 80psi and had a jib just under 25 feet long. This crane was renumbered C602 in 1936 and ended its days at Neasden Depot in 1970. C182, which had the makers number 917, was not renumbered by London Transport.

Steam crane at Stockwell depot, C&SLR. The crane became redundant on the completion of the enlarging of the tunnels. It may have been numbered C186 in the Underground numbering scheme.

61

Most depots and yards were provided with steam-powered rail-borne cranes to unload and load works trains and also, where necessary, to transfer material to and from road vehicles. While these cranes were mobile within the confines of the depots and the railway tracks on which they were placed, they were not truly travelling cranes, since they were mostly outside the normal running line loading gauge and had to be moved from one location to another by road as and when this was necessary. However, they were numbered within the series covering the travelling cranes. Cranes located in depot yards were only steamed when necessary, often standing cold for long periods and frequently had a very long life, being scrapped only when the steam boilers required extensive repairs or renewals. Mobile road cranes with sufficient capacity are now available for hire, to cover the odd occasions when such equipment is needed, so that depot-located steam cranes are no longer required.

Most of the steam yard cranes were of 5-ton capacity with boiler pressures between 80 and 100psi and with jibs from 25 to 35 feet in length. They were usually fitted with rudimentary couplings so that they could be towed about the yards when necessary, the steam power of the crane mainly being provided for lifting and slewing with self-propulsion confined to short distances at very low speed.

A Taylor & Hubbard 5-ton yard crane built in 1907 was bought secondhand in 1920 for use on the construction of the extension between Golders Green and Edgware. This crane, owned by the London Electric Railway, had a 25ft jib and steam pressure of 90psi, was numbered C184 in the Underground fleet and was stationed at Golders Green. In the 1936 renumbering scheme it became C603 and in 1939 was transferred to Highgate for lifting cable drums on and off wagons for the equipping of the Barnet Line. In 1965 this crane was deemed beyond economic repair and scrapped. It was replaced by C621 — also a 5-ton yard crane but built by Thomas Smith & Son in 1936 — which had been purchased from McAlpine in 1958 for use on the Metropolitan four-tracking work. By 1964, C621 stood idle at Rickmansworth, so there was no difficulty making it available for duty at Highgate to replace C603. However, after 1967 it was little used, and in 1971 it was taken to Lillie Bridge depot where a new boiler was fitted. This crane remained in active service in the yard at Lillie Bridge until 1983 when it was acquired by the Museum of London who currently have it in store.

The depots at Neasden, Lillie Bridge, Ealing Common, Northfields, Golders Green and Hainault were all provided with a 5-ton steam crane at one time or another. The equipment depot for the Northern Line extensions, located at Wellington Sidings, adjacent to what became known as Highgate Depot, also had cranes of this type provided. The cranes themselves were sometimes interchanged from location to location to cover repair and maintenance requirements.

The 5-ton crane C601 at Wood Lane was scrapped in 1937 and was replaced by a similar capacity Booth crane built in 1917, which had been purchased in 1936 and numbered C608. It had a jib 38 feet long and worked with a steam pressure of 100psi. It remained at Wood Lane until sold in 1958 after the depot ceased to be a main operating one. Central Line maintenance had, by then, been transferred to Ruislip Depot.

In 1937, to help with the 1935/40 New Works Programme, three four-wheeled cranes of 5-ton capacity were obtained secondhand to work at various locations. C609 was a Taylor & Hubbard crane with a 31ft jib and a working pressure of 90psi, C610 was a Grafton crane with a 27ft jib and a pressure of 100psi and C611 was a Thomas Smith and Sons crane with a 32ft jib and a working pressure also of 100psi. These cranes worked at such locations as Wood Lane, Draper's Field, Willesden Green, Hainault and Lillie Bridge.

A further three cranes of the yard type were obtained in 1938; C612 and C614 however were cranes with only 3-ton capacity, but had boiler pressures of 100psi. C612 had a jib of 35 feet while the jib of C614 was only 25 feet long. Both cranes were manufactured by Thomas Smith & Sons. The crane given the number in between — C613 — was a 5-ton Grafton, also with a boiler pressure of 100psi. This crane had a jib length of 34ft 7ins and was provided with RCH (Railway Clearing House) type couplings. None of the yard type cranes were fitted with wheel brakes.

Three yard cranes were loaned to the Great Western Railway during the war years, namely C609, C613 and C616.

C609 had been obtained originally for use at Draper's Field — the equipping depot for the eastern extension of the Central Line. During the war years it spent some time at Old Oak Common yard and survived until 1968 at Neasden Depot.

C613 had been obtained in 1938 for use at Wellington sidings but after being released from service on the Great Western Railway was returned to Ruislip Depot, subsequently doing service at Watford Tip. It was returned to Ruislip and scrapped in 1970.

C616 was a 5-ton Butler crane with a 42ft long jib and boiler pressure of 100psi and was obtained for use at Willesden Green — the equipment depot for the extension of the Bakerloo Line to Stanmore. C616 had been working in Llanelly in South Wales and was returned by the Great Western Railway to Draper's Field with the main frame broken in two pieces. However, a new casting was obtained and the crane was returned to service at Draper's Field for work on the Central Line eastern extension. Considerable correspondence ensued with the Western Region concerning the balance between the maintenance commitments and the repair costs before the problem was eventually solved C616 was transferred from Draper's Field to Ruislip in 1952 and subsequently had a new boiler fitted in 1964 and continued to work until recently — one of the last steam cranes in regular service.

The only other 5-ton steam yard crane which remained in active duty into the 1980s was C620, another Thomas Smith & Son crane built in 1926, but purchased secondhand from T.W. Ward Ltd in 1958 for use at Hainault Permanent Way Depot. This crane was obtained to replace C612, which had been seriously damaged in a derailment in the depot in June 1954 and had been pronounced beyond economic repair. The Permanent Way Depot at Hainault subsequently ceased to be generally active when new facilities, including the long welded rail depot, were installed at Ruislip at the other end of the line. Crane C620 was then re-located at Neasden Depot, where it remained until withdrawal in 1983.

Mobile yard steam crane C611 at Lillie Bridge. This was a five-ton crane built by Thomas Smith & Sons and acquired by London Transport in 1937. It was scrapped in 1973.

A 5 ton steam crane acquired by LT from T.W. Ward in 1958. It was originally built by Thomas Smith & Sons in 1926 and was withdrawn in 1981.

Cranes confined to yard duties were very useful for the transference of heavy and bulky materials on and off railway wagons but the most interesting vehicles are the truly travelling cranes which can be used on the railway tracks for complicated track renewals, bridge repairs and replacement, other heavy reconstruction work as well as attendance at breakdowns where appropriate.

The cranes which were moved about the railway in ballast trains to working sites on the railway tracks usually required attendant wagons to act as jib carriers.

The District Railway purchased a Grafton 5-ton travelling steam crane with works number 2077 in 1925. This crane worked at a steam pressure of 85psi and was provided with a very long jib of 35ft 6ins. It was not intended to be a breakdown crane but was required for general lifting duties about the railway. The crane was originally numbered C187 in the Underground fleet and because of the length of the jib required two carriers (or runners as they were sometimes called) when it was necessary to move the crane around the system. The nature of the work did not require the runners to be permanently coupled to the crane as they were only needed when the crane had to be moved within a ballast train to a particular site. Subsequently two ex-Metropolitan rail wagons RW450A and RW450B were modified to become jib carriers J686 and J687 for use with this crane, which had been renumbered C605 in the London Transport fleet.

Crane C605 sustained serious damage on two different occasions. In 1948 it ran away near South Harrow necessitating extensive repairs and almost 10 years later, in 1958, it was damaged at Lillie Bridge, when it sustained a cracked main frame which was subsequently repaired by the process known as 'Metalock'. A new boiler was fitted in 1960, and the crane with its jib carriers was transferred to Neasden to work in the permanent way yard, where it continued to work until 1983.

The District Railway also possessed a 10-ton travelling crane obtained in 1931 from Ransome & Rapier. This crane was originally numbered C189 but was renumbered C607 in the 1936 scheme. It had a 30ft jib and a boiler pressure of 120psi. After the formation of London Transport it was not normally required for breakdown duty, so it was transferred to permanent way work and was for a time retained at Lillie Bridge.

The crane itself was carried on three axles and was provided with a jib carrier numbered J685 (originally numbered J175), which was a four-wheeled vehicle having a 14ft wheelbase with the handbrake working on all four wheels. In June 1960 this crane was involved in a fatal accident at Farringdon when the jib was allowed to foul a bridge. In addition this accident caused serious damage to the crane so that it was decided to replace it, and in 1962 it was sold to Cox and Danks for scrap. Subsequently in 1963, J685 was also taken off the fleet list as being surplus to requirements and scrapped.

In 1933 London Transport inherited two travelling steam cranes, which had a lifting capacity of 30 tons. These cranes were capable of travelling over the system as part of a works train, and were therefore provided with jib carriers to run with them.

Crane C604 had been purchased in 1925 by the Metropolitan Railway from Cowan Sheldon, being used as a breakdown crane, manned by rolling stock personnel from Neasden Depot and normally kept in Neasden Yard.

It was an eight-wheeled steam crane with a boiler pressure of 100psi and jib length of 28ft 6ins and was usually made up in a breakdown train which consisted of one or more of the following vehicles, depending on the nature of the incident.

In the first place there was the jib carrier J682 which was a four-wheeled wagon of 6-tons capacity converted from an old ballast wagon which had been numbered 50 in the Metropolitan Railway fleet. Some records of the Metropolitan Railway indicated that wagons 31 to 50 were purchased secondhand in 1882. However, in the capital asset books, J682 was recorded as being of 1886 vintage. This jib carrier was replaced with an 8-ton ballast wagon dating from 1919 which was then renumbered J683. J682 was withdrawn for scrapping in 1968 after it had been used as an accommodation wagon at Lillie Bridge depot to hold steam engine boilers and other large fabrications while the rest of the locomotive was under repair in the workshop.

The breakdown train also contained two tool vans numbered BD700 and BD701 which had previously been Metropolitan Railway Milk Vans No. 3 and No. 5 respectively. These had been two of a fleet of six vehicles which had been attached to passenger trains to collect milk on the Aylesbury Line from such places as Wendover. BD701 was scrapped in 1944, but BD700 was restored at Neasden Depot as Milk Van No. 3 in Metropolitan Railway livery for the centenary celebrations in 1963. Subsequently this vehicle has been preserved at the London Transport Museum at Covent Garden in this condition. In addition the breakdown train could contain vehicles BD702 and BD703 which were both box vans though very different from each other. BD702 was a four-wheeled van converted from Metropolitan Railway ballast wagon BW195 in 1946, while BD703 was an eight-wheeled bogie van dating from 1910. These vans contained equipment, specialised tools and personnel accommodation for use at breakdowns when required. In 1937 an additional vehicle was added to this group to carry a spare emergency bogie. For this duty a four-wheeled ballast wagon, BW251, was modified to become a 10-ton flat wagon to take this breakdown bogie, which could be used for supporting either a tube or surface stock car. The vehicle was then renumbered BD704.

The vehicles were marshalled into a breakdown train as required, as the details of the incident requiring the attendance of the breakdown train became known.

With the transfer in 1937 of the Metropolitan Line steam service beyond Rickmansworth to the London and North Eastern Railway, the need for a heavy breakdown crane under the control of London Transport became less important. The Underground breakdown practice was based on jacking and packing to lift derailed vehicles. Such practice can often be time consuming but the alternative of positioning a crane at the site was often very difficult if not impossible to achieve. The rare occasions on the London Transport system on which a crane was essential was such that the retention of a crane specifically for the purpose was uneconomic. The decision was therefore taken to

Metropolitan Railway 50-ton crane at Neasden. It was built by Cowan Sheldon & Co in 1924.

Below Met Railway 50-ton crane in use at Neasden in LT days. This crane became C604 in 1937 and was scrapped in 1965.

The Breakdown Train vans: BD702 (the four-wheeled tool van), BD700 (the converted milk van No. 3), with BD703 (the eight wheeled non-bogie van) furthest from the camera.

65

scrap the crane retained specifically for breakdown purposes, because in emergency there would be time for any suitable crane to be requisitioned for the purpose. When the train was withdrawn in 1965, breakdown crane C604 and jib carrier J683 were despatched to South Wales for scrapping while BD703 and BD704 were broken up at Neasden.

The second of these two heavy cranes was one that the Metropolitan District Railway purchased from Ransome & Rapier in 1931 — a 30-ton crane which was subsequently numbered C606. Initially this was kept at Lillie Bridge, although later it was moved to Neasden, becoming the general heavy duty crane for permanent way work. At 27 feet, the jib of this crane was about a foot shorter than that of the Cowan Sheldon crane C604. It was provided with a jib carrier numbered J684, which had a hand brake working on all four wheels. It was used mainly for civil engineering work on location when bridge repairs were necessary, and for loading engineering trains with heavy equipment.

In 1976 arrangements were made to convert this crane from steam to diesel and this conversion was carried out by Cowan & Sheldon at Carlisle, being completed in 1978. In the rebuilding, the original steam engine and boiler were removed and replaced by a diesel engine with a torque converter and gearbox. This was connected by bevel gearing to the former steam-engine crank shaft which drove the crane. The crane machinery itself thus remained virtually unaltered. However, the control was modified so that clutches which were formerly hand-operated through mechanical linkages were converted to direct operation by compressed air cylinders. In addition, various safety devices were added to bring the crane control and operation up to modern requirements, including safe-load indicators using load cells and electrically controlled meters to warn of overloads at all states of slewing and lifting. The crane was capable of hoisting, slewing and travelling within certain limitations. The diesel engine had four cylinders developing 85bhp at 1800rpm, and considerable sound-proofing was included in the walls of the engine compartment. The torque converter was close-coupled to the engine flywheel and provided for high starting torques and overloads.

Although the conversion of this crane made it a most versatile heavy duty crane for railway work, the maximum load was only 30 tons at 12ft minimum radius. The crane had a lift of 23 feet above rail level to 16 feet below rail level at minimum radius and when on travel could move 15 tons at 2¼mph when required. Unfortunately this crane became seriously defective in 1982, which necessitated further expensive repairs. It was therefore decided to arrange for its replacement by a Cowan & Sheldon 7½-ton crane.

The original jib carrier J684 which ran with this crane was scrapped after a new runner was provided by the conversion of the old welding plant well wagon WPW1001 at Acton Works. After conversion this wagon was renumbered J683 — the second time this number had been used for a jib carrier — and was finished in yellow livery to match the new colour scheme adopted for the reconditioned crane.

With the withdrawal of steam locomotives from active service the skilled maintenance required for steam cranes also disappeared and as the steam cranes required major repairs they were withdrawn from service.

In 1954, two specially designed diesel-electric travelling jib cranes were ordered for general use in the system. A particular feature of the design of these cranes was the requirement that, with their jib carriers, they should be capable of being hauled in engineering works trains through the tube tunnels, which had not been possible with the large steam cranes.

Before these cranes (which were numbered C617 and C618) were obtained, over 100 miles of track in the open were being maintained, on which a crane could have been usefully employed but which could not be reached over London Transport rails by existing steam cranes. Part of this trackage could be reached by established connections with British Railways without traversing tube tunnels. Some of these connections were subsequently removed and this made access of special equipment more difficult. The two connections concerned were that at Leyton (where there was the original connection with the Eastern Region of BR giving access to the Eastern section of the Central Line) and that at Highgate Wood Sidings (reached from Finsbury Park over the Barnet Line).

The design parameters of the crane were difficult because in addition to the loading gauge problems, the specification called for a lift of six tons at 16ft radius, while the axle load was not to exceed 13 tons unloaded. The design produced by Taylor & Hubbard included articulation of the foot of the jib for the negotiation of curves in the tunnels while in transit on engineering trains. The articulation is provided automatically in the lowered position, when the jib has been secured on the jib carrier.

The jib carriers were provided by London Transport and were specially altered flat wagons, the conversion work being undertaken at Acton Works. When completed the vehicles were numbered J688 and J689. They were identical and could be transferred between cranes, so that neither one was associated with a particular crane. The 25-ton flat wagons used for the purpose were F308 and F309, built in 1925.

The re-engagement of the equipment for operation of the crane is automatic after the release of the jib from the carrier. The crane itself is built on an underframe carried on three axles having plain axle bearings. The weight of the crane and ultimately its load is distributed between the three axles, the middle pair of wheels being flangeless to prevent fouling of the check rails on curves of minimum radius.

Hoisting, derricking, slewing and travelling are arranged by means of independent 600-volt motors driving through appropriate reduction gearing. The control gear is cam-operated with appropriate safety interlocking.

A McLaren three-cylinder 75hp diesel engine, running at 1000rpm and driving a 50kW compound-wound direct current generator manufactured by the Lancashire Dynamo & Crypto Co, supplies the electrical power. The diesel engine has only two controlled speeds, idling and full speed.

Another important feature of the design is that the jib had to be capable of slewing round a complete revolution with a tail radius that would clear trackside cable posts and platform copings at the extremes of the track loading gauge.

30-ton Ransome & Rapier steam crane at Lillie Bridge in August 1931 shortly after delivery. It is now C606, having been converted to diesel operation in 1978 and repainted in yellow livery.

Left Crane C606 after conversion to diesel operation, seen at work at Neasden depot during the scrapping of four-wheeled hopper wagons. Right A Taylor & Hubbard diesel-electric crane with jib fully raised and with one buffer in stowed position and the other lowered.

The crane end of a jib carrier modified to work with diesel electric cranes, showing the close coupling arrangements with Ward coupler, solid side buffers and centre drawhook.

The diesel generator set is mounted on the superstructure. The power supply to the various motors can either be provided from this generator or obtained from the 600-volt traction supply at the current rails by means of collector shoes, which can be placed on an adjacent track and connected to a power socket on the crane underframe. The 600-volt supply can therefore be obtained without the track on which the crane itself is working being alive.

The main frames of the cranes are provided at both ends with Ward type automatic couplings at tube height and RCH drawgear with hinged buffers for coupling with main line vehicles, similar to those provided on battery locomotives. Movement from location to location can therefore be arranged by various motive power units and in different train formation as convenient.

The jib itself is swan-necked and of rolled steel channel, being 37 feet long. It can lift up to 5½ tons at 15ft radius, decreasing to the 35ft radius at full extension, while standing free on the rail. Arrangements can be made to block the crane to reduce the possibility of tipping, so that increased loads at extended radii can be lifted.

The crane can traverse under the control of the travelling motor with a 5-ton load. Crane safety devices are incorporated, including a safe load indicator connected to the derrick rope which gives both a visible and an audible warning of overload conditions. Limit switches prevent hoisting and derricking from exceeding the safe limit. The controls for the safety gear are actuated by a 24-volt battery, not dependent (except for recharging) on the main power supply. An automatic electric horn is sounded when the crane begins travel movement. In addition there is a light cluster, arranged to illuminate the load and hoisting movement, so that work at night is not difficult to control.

These cranes were very successful and met a long-felt need for engineering maintenance work, so that in 1964 another unit was ordered from Taylor & Hubbard, requiring the conversion of a further jib carrier at Acton Works. The new crane was numbered C622 and the jib carrier J691, the latter having been converted from flat wagon F312.

In February 1982, the first of four additional cranes was delivered to Lillie Bridge from Cowan & Sheldon. These diesel-hydraulic cranes (C623-626) of 7½-ton capacity with a telescopic jib do not require a jib carrier but are mounted on two four-wheeled bogies. The need for large cranes capable of carrying out all conceivable jobs has never been great, but now has reduced considerably. A larger number of smaller capacity cranes capable of reaching the whole system is more necessary and when a heavy lift is unavoidable, specialist equipment can be hired from contractors. In addition, however, a twin jib track relaying crane (C627) was purchased from Cowan & Sheldon in 1986.

Recently acquired is this Cowan Sheldon 7½-ton diesel crane with telescopic jib that does not require a jib carrier.

Permanent Way Vehicles

The track of the London Underground railway system is laid to standard gauge of 4ft 8½ins, and the electrical collection arrangement is that known as the four-rail insulated return system requiring, in addition to the two running rails, two conductor rails with top surface contact by collector shoes carried on the rolling stock. This system is almost unique to London Transport and was developed originally to avoid earth current leakage problems affecting other public utilities, such as telephones, water and gas supplies. The Mersey Railway was originally provided with a four-rail system similar to the Metropolitan District in London in 1904, but was subsequently converted by British Railways to third-rail. The Milan Underground Line 1 has a four-rail system, but the outside positive rail has a side contact collection arrangement.

Both the conductor rails are supported on porcelain insulators, the rail placed outside the running rails being the positive conductor and the rail in the centre of the track the negative conductor. The running rails in the Underground for many years were mainly of the British Standard bullhead type but in recent years new track has been laid with flat bottomed Vignoles section rail, because the steel rolling mills were no longer willing to produce short runs of bullhead rail just for London Transport.

Rail lengths are dictated by a number of factors, but London Transport were pioneers in the provision of long welded rails. The normal length of the rails as delivered was 60 feet but they were welded into 300 foot lengths before laying. Before 1960 London Transport had installed a greater mileage of long welded rails than British Railways.

In 1937 a welding machine was installed at Lillie Bridge Depot to flash-butt weld rail lengths together. This machine was in constant use until 1946, the completed welded lengths of rail being transferred to the laying site by special trains made up of long flat wagons.

At the same time arrangements were made for a mobile plant to be constructed so that flash butt welding could be carried out on site or near the location where re-railing was in progress. Two special wagons WPW1000 and WPW1001 were constructed at Acton Works to meet these requirements.

WPW1000 was fitted with a diesel generator to provide the welding power and WPW1001 was constructed as a well wagon to contain the flash butt welder. The vehicles were so constructed that they remained within the tube loading gauge and could therefore be transferred to any site on the system.

The flash-butt welding plant on these vehicles was used intermittently at various sites as required. It was found however, that better control of the welding could be achieved at the welding plant at Lillie Bridge, so the mobile set became only a back up to the delivery of most of the 300 foot lengths of rails to the site by a long welded rail train. At one stage however, the mobile set was loaned to the Southern Region to help with the Bournemouth electrification, for welding the new conductor rail. After the completion of this work the two vehicles were transferred to Willesden Green sidings, used as a Permanent Way Storage Depot, but after 1972 this mobile plant was not used again and subsequently the wagons were removed for scrapping. Their useful life was however not yet over.

Diesel generator wagon for mobile rail welding plant on the traverser at Acton works, where it was constructed in 1937.

WPW1001, the flat wagon, was converted in 1975 at Acton Works into the jib carrier J683 for use with the diesel-converted crane, while WPW1000 was converted to a bogie well wagon.

In 1947 a new static flash-butt welder was installed in a specially prepared shop at Lillie Bridge Depot. A more modern installation was provided at Ruislip Depot in 1969 to replace the installation at Lillie Bridge. All rail welding work now takes place in a purpose-built plant at Ruislip and trains now leave this depot loaded with rails for various points on London Underground's rail system. To assist the distribution of rails throughout the whole of the Underground railway system, a connecting loop was installed between the depot located on the Central Line and the Uxbridge branch of the Metropolitan Line. This loop line, only used for the transfer of works trains and empty passenger stock, was brought into service on 24th July 1973.

The welded rails are transported to the working sites on five rail wagons coupled together to make a train hauled originally by steam engine but later only by battery locomotives. The original load for the trains on this work was limited to eight 300ft lengths of rail. At Lillie Bridge the loading was carried out relatively simply, achieved by means of an overhead gantry crane installed in the welding shop, which not only serviced the welder itself but stacked, stored and loaded the finished lengths of rail

After the second world war there were 53 rail wagons, each of 20 tons capacity, in the London Transport fleet. It should be noted that rail wagons are longer than flat wagons because rolled rails are 60 feet long before welding. The rail wagons, which had various building dates (the earliest being 1931), were used for conveying rails until 1958, when a specially designed train consisting of five wagons constructed by the Gloucester Railway Carriage & Wagon Company Ltd was ordered.

These wagons, numbered RW490-RW494, were normally kept together as a rake. The underframes and bogies were of a similar type to those of the previous rail wagons, but RW490 was specially equipped with a winch and control mechanism and also provided with through power and communication cables.

This train was designed to convey 18 long welded rails in one transhipment; this load being stacked in three tiers, the bottom tier being supported by bolsters which were bolted to the deck plates of the wagons and spaced just over eight feet apart. Loose bolsters, provided to separate the tiers from each other, had locking pins to prevent them from moving. The rails had to be given some freedom for sideways movement so that the train could negotiate curves. Vertical steel bars of heavy channel section fitted to the wagon solebars at each bolster location prevented the movement of the rails beyond the wagon deck. In addition, the bolsters positioned at the king pins of the wagons (about which the wagon truck movement takes place) held the rails in position laterally and symmetrically about the centre line of the train. These controls were designed to bring the rails back into line when the train formation returned to a straight track from a curve. On the middle rail wagon a clamping bar was provided holding the rails rigidly at the centre of their total length, so that at this point they were not free to move across the bolsters. This was in fact the only position on the train where the load was rigidly secured. The train was originally designed to deal with bullhead rail but modification of the pinning and securing clamps has been carried out so that flat-bottomed rail can also be accommodated.

The removal of the rails to the track is easily effected, either longitudinally off the end over the end roller by fixing the rail ends to the existing track and moving the train from under it, or sideways by a permanent way gang. However the special feature of the equipment provided on this train was a means of lifting rails up from the track. Previously when 300ft lengths of rail or even shorter lengths had to be replaced the rails removed had to be cut to lengths which could be manhandled on to the rail wagons. The recovered rails could not then be used again for further periods of service at other, less vulnerable, locations where some rail wear could be tolerated.

The loading of the rails from the track was carried out by an 8hp electric winch carried on the trailing end of the last and special wagon RW490. This wagon was placed close to the end of the rail to be lifted, a roller with a special frame being swung into position over the wagon headstock. The rail end was then lifted and placed on the roller by the winch. A special guide rope was attached and the train propelled under the rail until the last 20 feet was left overhanging the end, when the winch was again used to place the rail finally on the train. The train could load one tier of rails on a curve not exceeding 20 chains. The time to load one 300 foot length of rail was about 8 minutes.

The guard in charge of the train operated from the winch end of the train and had telephone communication with the driver of the battery locomotive at the leading end. The winch wagon supply lines and inter-communications lines were taken down the train through an additional 10-point control line. Four of the fleet of battery locomotives, L56-L59, were originally provided with the facilities to meet this arrangement but the later locomotives L20-L32 were also equipped and one of these locomotives had to be provided on this train at the end remote from the winch wagon if the winch was to be used.

The rail wagons were of course close coupled by means of Ward couplings of the tube type with central buffers, but did not have additional RCH couplers as most other wagons did.

A special long welded rail train made up with these vehicles hauled by Battery Locomotive L57 gave a demonstration of loading and unloading 300ft rails at the Underground Centenary Parade at Neasden Depot on Thursday 23rd May 1963.

The train could be moved by steam locomotive provided that rail loading was not required, but to enable transfer to the working site to be achieved by steam locomotive it was necessary to provide brake vans at either end of the rake of rail wagons. As standard brake vans were normally fitted with RCH buffers and couplings, two special brake vans, with Ward couplings at one end to couple to the rail train, had to be provided.

The two brake vans (FB578 and FB579) which had been used with DEL120 were now selected to form brake vans for the long welded rail train, thus undergoing further conversion. A full-width cab replaced the sentry boxes, and scrap rails were placed

Below **The classic photograph of long-welded rail train at Lillie Bridge depot, showing the disposition of 300ft length rails on curves and crossings.**

Right **Demonstration of the unloading of long-welded rails from the flat cars by means of anchored chains and train movement.**

Below right **The long-welded rail train from the rear-end wagon. RW490 is fitted with an electric hoist and roller system for lifting 300ft long rails from the track.**

beneath to increase the tare weight of the vehicles to 18 tons. At the cab end hinged RCH buffers similar to those provided on battery locomotives were fitted which could be swung out of use if necessary.

The Westinghouse brake equipment originally fitted was removed as it was not required for working with steam locomotives. The handbrake, however, was provided with additional leverage to match the increase in tare weight. The Westinghouse main and train line air pipes were retained to enable the vehicles to be marshalled if necessary in a fully braked train.

The cab was fitted with a small coal-fired stove and locker space along the inner bulkhead. These lockers actually doubled as seats. It was possible to carry a small amount of material (up to 2 tons) on each of these vans. After conversion they were branded "to be used only as brake vans with steam locomotives".

A further 12 rail wagons were purchased from British Rail Workshops in 1965. Ten of these wagons, which were numbered RW495-RW506, were formed into two five-vehicle rail wagon trains for conveying 300ft rail lengths, but none of these vehicles were provided with a winch and so unloading had to be performed manually. These wagons were arranged to be close coupled with Ward coupling gear but only the ends of the vehicles at the outer ends of the rakes were provided with main line buffing gear to permit coupling to steam locomotives. The main line buffers can be hinged back so that coupling by Ward can be arranged if necessary.

The introduction of long welded rails on the track requires a controlled system of destressing when the ambient temperature varies markedly within a short space of time. If a long cold spell of weather is followed by a sudden increase in ambient temperature, destressing problems can arise.

In order to combat this trouble, a rail-warming trolley has been provided which can be used to ensure that the rail temperature is controlled while destressing is being carried out before the long welded rail is locked up into position.

The trolley is moved by manpower and carries bottles of propane gas which provide the heating fuel. Its use is confined to those periods when the ambient temperature is not satisfactory for proper destressing. The trolley was constructed by D. Wickham & Co. Ltd to the requirements of London Transport.

Where intensive multiple unit train services are operated, the permanent way engineer has to contend with the problem of rail corrugation. One method of trying to save rails from the need for early renewal where such corrugations become bad is to grind the surface of the rail to remove the corrugation and to restore a smooth surface.

In 1931 an ex-Bakerloo Gate Stock trailer car, numbered 1575 in the old numbering scheme and which had been replaced by the introduction of air door stock, was converted for rail grinding duty. The car seating was removed, the interior was equipped with water tanks and appropriate pipework to lubricate the carborundum grinding blocks fitted to the bogies. This converted car was at first given the number RG207, but subsequently in the 1936 renumbering scheme it became RG800 and about this time a second vehicle was similarly converted. This was also an ex-Bakerloo gate stock trailer car, 1574, and when converted in 1936 it was re-numbered RG801. These two cars had been built in 1906 by the American Car and Foundry Company, being numbered 208 and 209 originally, renumbered in 1926 to 1574 and 1575 and then withdrawn from passenger service in 1930. The bodies after a further 20 years additional service on rail grinding duty became a maintenance liability. These vehicles normally worked out of Lillie Bridge depot marshalled between two ballast motor cars to provide the motive power, and would grind the rails concerned by making several short passes over each section to be treated, so that track possession was essential.

Two 1923 Tube Stock trailer cars were reserved from the 1949 tube rolling stock replacement programme for conversion to rail grinding cars to replace the two original cars, RG800 and RG801. The cars selected for conversion were 75241 and 75245, both of which had started life as control trailers. They had been 'demobbed' in 1939 — a term applied to the conversion of control trailers to plain trailers — by leaving the driving cab denuded of equipment, when their operation as control trailer cars was being discontinued. The prefix 7 was added to the original car number when this conversion was completed. When converted to rail grinders they were renumbered RG802 and RG803, becoming available for duty in 1956.

After the seating had been removed they were each fitted with six water tanks having a total capacity of 1800 gallons. The tanks were equipped with filler pipes on either side of the vehicles so that when the vehicles were turned round in the course of their duty, the refilling of the tanks could still be achieved at an appropriate water stand pipe. The original bulkheads for the driver's compartments, which had not been removed when the conversion to trailers had been arranged, were now removed and the side doors sealed up.

The actual grinding was accomplished by rectangular aluminium oxide grinding blocks mounted in shoes on the bogies and applied to the running rails by pneumatically operated cylinders. The brake gear and other appendages on the truck frames were removed to permit the fitting of the grinding shoe assemblies and the operating cylinders. The grinding blocks were returned to the clear position by the action of springs, but the grinding action was produced by compressed air pressure available from the main line pipe provided by the ballast motors for the Westinghouse brake system, although the rail grinding cars themselves were unbraked. Six grinding shoes were located at three positions on each side of each bogie, one at each end under the bogie headstock and one centrally under the bolster. Those at the outer ends of the bogies contained two grinding blocks, while the central location contained four blocks. Water sprays were arranged to eject water in front of the grinding blocks in the direction of travel, control being achieved manually by an operator located inside the car.

The normal working arrangement was for the two rail grinding cars to be coupled together between two ballast motor cars, so forming a four-car unit. By experience the most efficient speed for grinding was found to be about 20mph. As the work was carried out under night track possessions the unit could be passed to and fro at this speed over the section of rails to be treated.

Above **Rail grinding car RG207, converted from ex-Bakerloo gate stock trailer 1575. It was renumbered RG800 in 1936 and scrapped in 1955. Below left** A close-up of the grinding blocks mounted on the bogies of RG207. Water pipes were fitted to the blocks to assist the grinding process.

Above right **Interior of one of the Pre-1938 stock rail grinding cars showing the water tanks. During the late 1960s these vehicles were used for leaf-clearing on the western branches of the Piccadilly Line. Below Rail grinding cars RG802 and RG803, converted from control trailers 75241 and 75245 and completed in 1956. These cars were originally 1923 Metro control trailers built for the Hampstead Line and numbered 751 and 755, later becoming 5241 and 5245 in the 1930 renumbering scheme.**

Another important miscellaneous requirement associated with the permanent way is that of gauging. Constructional work and rearrangements of equipment are constantly being undertaken on a railway so that it is necessary to ensure that in consequence the loading gauge is not infringed. This is achieved by passing over the track at regular intervals, a gauging car proving the accepted dimensions. The early gauging cars were usually normal passenger rolling stock provided with special lead fingers placed at strategic points on the profile of the vehicle. However the need for a specialised vehicle for this purpose became evident from an early date because of the necessity to observe in some detail the very limited clearances required in the tube tunnels.

In 1922, to assist in the inspection of the enlarged tunnel work being undertaken on the City and South London Railway, an old LER flat wagon was made up as a gauging car and was subsequently given the number G661. This vehicle was scrapped in 1936.

A new tube gauging car was provided at about this time by conversion from flat wagon F124. This wagon was then given the number G660. The vehicle had girdle frame bogies and when it was scrapped after nearly 30 years of intermittent service, it had a French-built trailer bogie at one end and an American built bogie at the other, both of this so-called 'girdle frame' pattern.

Another tube type gauging car was provided in 1963 and numbered G663. This was obtained by converting at Acton Works 1931 Tube Stock trailer car No. 7131, built originally by the Birmingham Carriage and Wagon Company for the Piccadilly Line.

A surface type gauging car was produced in 1934 from the underframe of a Metropolitan car built in 1906 by the Metropolitan Amalgamated Railway, Carriage & Wagon Co. This gauging vehicle was numbered G662 but was scrapped in 1980 when G663, the tube stock vehicle, was adapted to cover both surface and tube line gauging.

A City & South London car underframe on which a gauging frame was fitted for checking the enlarged tunnels. The fingers are electrical contacts which are broken when contact with an obstruction is made.

A Metropolitan Railway car underframe of 1904 vintage. It would appear to have been set up to check the profile of the 1923 Gloucester type cars of the District for clearances.

Surface line gauging car G662, made from an old Metropolitan Railway coaching stock underframe in 1934. This gauging car was withdrawn and scrapped in 1980.

Tube stock gauging car G663, converted in 1963 from one-time LER tube stock car 7131 built in 1931.

The maintenance of permanent way was traditionally a job requiring considerable manpower until the advent of mechanical tamping machines which enabled some of the arduous manual work to be mechanised. London Transport however was at a disadvantage with the four-rail track system having the positive outside current rail so close to the running rails as well as a centre conductor rail.

In 1959 a Plasser-Theurer ballast tamper was obtained in connection with the new four-tracking work, north of Harrow-on-the-Hill, and this machine was later tried on other duties in connection with permanent way maintenance. Its operation on the four-rail system proved successful and three similar machines were obtained in 1966. PBT760 was the number given to the first unit, which was withdrawn in 1970, and the three subsequent ones were numbered PBT761-PBT763.

Being provided with hydraulic jacks these machines were able to be turned round on each track and to be lifted so that they could be off-set on to specially prepared stabling sites. In this way they were not required to return 'home' after each spell of duty, so that their working time on site, which is always severely limited in any event by the service requirements, could be maximised.

A special track lining machine numbered PTL764 was added to the fleet in 1973 and in 1975 a points and crossing tamping machine, SC765, was obtained because the original machines could not deal with complicated track work involved at points and crossings. Maintenance at these places had still needed gangs of men. SC765 is self-propelled and can work to and from the working site on its own.

In 1980 a further three tamping machines numbered TMM771-773 were delivered from Plasser-Theurer of Austria to replace the machines obtained in 1966. These new machines are very sophisticated and incorporate the latest control features for permanent way maintenance.

Left Plasser-Theurer tamper type VKR05 stabled on its special trackside site at Kilburn adjacent to the northbound Metropolitan Line. The tamping end of the vehicle is away from the camera. It is one of three vehicles built in 1966 and recently withdrawn. **Right** One of the 1980 (type PU0716) tamping machines which were numbered TMM771-773.

This is London Transport's only Plasser-Theurer switch and crossing tamping machine. It is numbered SC765 and it is designed to move to its working site under its own power.

TRC666, converted from 1973 stock trailer car 514 for insertion between the two Cravens motor cars. This replaced an earlier plan to use ex-1938 stock trailer 012331, converted to become TRC912 in 1978 but never used. TRC666 is very smartly turned out in red, grey and black and is seen at Bedford during delivery from BREL's Derby carriage works in May 1987.

With the mechanisation of track maintenance it was necessary to provide some measure of the track condition both before and after treatment and to check the need for reconditioning work. In 1964, five out of the six 1960 Tube Stock four-car units were converted at Acton Works for the experimental automatic train operation. The unit containing car numbers 3910-4902-4903-3911 was not converted at this time and in 1971 was transferred to Service Stock duties as a track testing unit. It was provided with instruments to record track information and periodically it travelled over the whole of the London Transport railway system. In 1977 this unit was sent for an overhaul to Acton Works. However, the two trailer cars 4902 and 4903, which had originally been Pre-1938 Tube Stock trailer cars, were not to be overhauled but replaced by a single 1938 Tube Stock trailer, 012331. This was converted for track recording work and renumbered TRC912. The 1960 Tube Stock motor cars at the same time were allocated, but never carried, the numbers TRC910 and TRC911 in place of 3910 and 3911 respectively. They were not painted, retaining their original unpainted aluminium finish. Unfortunately these Cravens built cars had been treated when constructed with sound deadening material to reduce the noise to the passengers and this contained asbestos in fairly large quantities. During the extensive refit at Acton this was considered to be a serious health hazard, and after a period of suspension of work the renovation was abandoned and this track testing unit never returned to service. Instrumentation has since been arranged on passenger stock of various types as and when such testing is required.

The idea of having a track recording unit to analyse the track work necessary is still felt important. Consequently trials have been made with BR track recording vehicles which are far more sophisticated than anything previously used on London's Underground. These have been used at regular intervals over as much of the system as is accessible by them. As a result a new Underground track recording unit is being provided by BREL using the BR equipment mounted on a redundant 1973 tube stock trailer car (514) to be hauled by two 1960 Tube Stock motor cars converted as pilot motors.

Another problem which requires attention on the running lines in tube tunnels is that of cleaning. The action of the steel wheels on the rails and the friction brake blocks create an enormous amount of dust which, because the tunnels are not subjected to the action of the weather, accumulates. It is therefore necessary from time to time to remove such accumulations.

Tunnel line cleaning wagon TLC2, converted from a 10-ton ballast wagon in 1948. These wagons were part of a train which toured the system and carried staff who cleaned the tunnel telephone wires by hand as they stood on the floor of the wagon.

A gang, composed mainly of women known as 'fluffers', were engaged on general cleaning of the track and the lower part of the tube tunnel walls and this gang progressed through the tube tunnels as required. In addition, a train was provided with equipment to clean the tunnel telephone wires which, being part of the safety equipment employed on London's Underground, must be kept in a condition which ensures good electrical contact. These wires are used in three ways; firstly when pinched together in an emergency, the power on the track is discharged, after which an emergency telephone can be clipped to the wires and an emergency conversation established between the driver and the power control. In addition a system known as Drico was developed which enabled the driver to clip a different telephone to the wires and communicate with the traffic controller without removing the traction current supply. Some of these arrangements are being replaced by more sophisticated systems of communications that are now available.

The 'fluffers' operation however, a job without much glamour, has been replaced by the provision of a tunnel cleaning train specially built for the purpose. This train of five cars was completed in 1977. The two outer end driving cars were converted from 1938 Tube Stock driving motor cars. 10226 became TCC1 and 10087 became TCC5, while TCC2, TCC3, and TCC4 were specially constructed to provide the special suction equipment and settling tanks for the dust collected.

One of the technical problems associated with providing such a train was controlling it at a slow enough speed to clean effectively the area being treated.

On TCC1 the conventional electric traction equipment used on 1938 Tube Stock was retained, but in addition a hydraulic drive was provided for slow speed operation with its own selector switch type controller. This selector switch provides for four speeds, 0.5mph, 1.5mph, 4.5mph and 6mph. In addition, a Permanent Way operator's cabin is provided to control the tunnel cleaning equipment. The car itself carries a suction fan and an exhaust chamber to pass clean air back into the tunnel together with the appropriate control equipment.

Car TCC5 is similar to TCC1 except that it is not equipped with slow speed drive equipment but has a selector switch so that the slow speed control can be exercised when driving from this car. A motor alternator to provide auxiliary power for the train is fitted.

TCC2 and TCC4 cars carry the dust compartments and filter chambers. Each car has built-in conveyors which unload the collected dust by way of discharge tubes into containers external to the train at appropriate depots. A safety feature is arranged to ensure that these discharge tubes are properly stowed before the train can be moved.

TCC3, the centre car of the train, carries the air nozzle equipment. The central blowing nozzles are fed by a fan with a low pressure but high velocity air flow which disturbs the dust, and the dust-laden air is then drawn into the system on either side by suction nozzles, this air passing to the filter chambers through large connecting tubes. The train is thus able to remove dust in either direction of travel.

There are approximately 160 miles of deep-level tube tunnel and provided the system works successfully, over the years it is anticipated that a pass will be made about once per year. However, until the accumulated dust has been removed, this circulation may not be achieved. This train is the first in the world to cover the cleaning of more than the track. It also cleans the walls and the dirt accumulated on cables and other wall mounted equipment. Tunnel cleaning trains are provided on other underground systems with varying amounts of success. It is hoped that in London the accumulation of dust will have been reduced by the introduction of trains with rheostatic braking, because the dust emanating from the destruction of brake blocks is reduced.

The cleaning train is driven at a constant very slow speed when operating and special hydraulic motors had to be provided to achieve this. Consideration was given to the employment of the metadyne principle to the conventional motors to give the slow speed but it was considered that this system would be even more complicated than the development of equipment specially, by utilising a hydraulic system already available in other fields. The filter bags can hold up to 6 tons of dust before returning to depot for discharge and special precautions have been taken to prevent or combat fires should they occur. The filter cars are divided into sections each with a sensor which gives a visual and audible warning in the operations cabin when a fire occurs. The fans and dust collecting operation are automatically stopped should one of these warnings occur. Fire fighting equipment using CO_2 gas is available both automatically and at the discretion of the operator, as well as the automatic release of a water mist. Otherwise the safety features associated with conventioinal passenger trains (apart from through access) are incorporated in the train.

The train is provided with Wedglock automatic type coupling heads at the outer ends for mechanical coupling only, so through brake and control lines are provided and an adaptor is required if coupling to a Ward or Buckeye is necessary. Ward/Wedglock and D-to-D/Wedglock coupling adaptors are provided as part of the train's emergency equipment.

In addition to the Westinghouse brake the train has been fitted with hydraulic parking brakes.

The train first went into trial tunnel cleaning service in 1978, but considerable problems arose which took time to eliminate. The train became fully operational in 1980.

Facing page captions

Top **The completed tunnel cleaning train, converted from 1938 tube stock between 1972 and 1977.**

Centre left **Rear of TCC1 showing air tunnel connectors.**

Centre right **TCC2 showing the discharge tube stowed below the solebar and the fire indicator lights on the outside of each of the filter chambers.**

Bottom left **The connections between TCC2 and TCC3.**

Bottom right **The centre pressure and suction openings for the cleaning cycle. The blower nozzles are in the centre and the suction nozzles on either side.**

79

AUTUMN & WINTER WORKING

The weather in England is very unpredictable and there is a wide variation in winter conditions from one year to the next and even from one day to the next. The winter and even the autumn can vary from mild dry weather to arctic conditions, and changes can take place overnight from one extreme to the other. The permutations and combinations produce all kinds of problems for operating an electric railway which depends on picking up the current supply from an exposed conductor rail. Over the London Transport area there can be considerable differences in conditions on the same day.

It is the surface sections of the railway which are vulnerable to winter conditions. In winter it is always 'warmer down below' so that it is only above ground that points freeze, snow blocks the lines, the current rail becomes coated with non-conducting ice and the moisture carried in the compressed air system, both in the trains and in the signalling equipment, freezes and stops valves and operating gear from working.

The high moisture content (the humidity) of the air in this country is such that when air is compressed, large quantities of water are deposited. Modern train equipment requires a lot of compressed air and in winter special precautions have to be taken to prevent this deposited water from freezing in vulnerable situations. Settling reservoirs are provided which have to be bled off and treated with some form of anti-freeze. No matter how detailed the precautions, some moisture passes into the system and under extreme conditions this causes valves to freeze and trains to be cancelled. Some additional protection can be gained by ensuring that the trains are stabled overnight in a shed. When the Victoria Line, for example, was planned as a totally underground line, with only the train depot and stabling area in the open, it was decided that all trains must be stabled inside sheds. Until this time, 75% of all operating rolling stock on most lines was stabled in the open.

At two very vulnerable depots, Cockfosters and Hainault, protection was provided by building draught screens, sheltering the trains from cold east winds.

It is essential to arrange some precautions during the period of inclement weather (which is considered to be from October to April), but these precautions should only be invoked on the basis of some sort of forecast. Agreement was therefore reached with the London Weather Centre for information to be passed to the Railway Traffic Controllers, who could then disseminate the information to those sections of the system which required the warning. However, all this only became essential after the tube railways began to run overground to the outer suburbs.

The District and Metropolitan Railways, even after electrification, did not experience current collection problems in cold and icy weather unless there were heavy falls of snow. Snow ploughs fitted to steam locomotives were brought into use whenever conditions were severe enough, but these were rarely used south of the Chilterns. The main reason for the fewer current collection problems on the surface railways with a four-rail system was that the trains were provided with power bus lines so that all the collector shoes of the same polarity were connected together and any one which made contact enabled the whole train to obtain power. The shoes leading tended to clear the current rails so that those at the rear of the train were able to pick up. Even the steam stock hauled by electric locomotives on the Metropolitan was provided with through bus lines, including collector shoes on the brake vans at the extreme ends of six or seven vehicle rakes. By this means electric locomotives were assured of power supply when traversing complicated points and crossings with their inevitable current rail gaps and this feature was invaluable under icing conditions. In the winter of 1925/26 there were severe snow conditions with low temperatures in London and some positive action was necessary to combat the weather. Apart from the use of snow scrapers and brushes, another idea which met with some success was tried by the District Railway, namely the spreading of warm oil over the surface of the current rails to prevent the formation of ice.

In addition to snow ploughs, which were only used very occasionally, the railways with tracks exposed to bad weather were provided with vehicles known as 'Sleet Wagons'. These were usually four-wheeled wagons converted for the purpose, being fitted with sleet brushes to scrape the current rails, both negative and positive. They were also provided with serrated rollers for crushing ice which had formed, and carried tanks containing liquid for spraying on the rails.

The fluid used was calcium chloride which had to be forced through the nozzles above the current rails by compressed air obtained from the main compressor line of the motive power unit. In about 1934 a proprietary fluid called 'Kilfrost', based on the anti-freeze material ethylene glycol became available in commercial quantities and, as this could be applied by gravity, neither compressed air nor heating were any longer required. Subsequent developments were based on using this type of material.

The Sleet Wagons were usually conveyed to the sites concerned between passenger motor cars specially selected for the duty. In 1936 there were nine of these vehicles, by that time numbered SW810-818.

Left Early type of sleet wagon between two gate stock motor cars at Golders Green depot. The Hampstead Line had two of these vehicles delivered in 1925 and 1927. **Right** Sleet equipment on early tube stock sleet wagon. Unlike the modern gear, the brushes and ice crushers were lowered by hand not by pneumatic cylinder, the brush gear having adjusting locations to take up the wear on the brush spikes.

The Metropolitan Railway had four such vehicles, which were numbered 213-226-236-300 in the Metropolitan fleet, and this would indicate that, with the exception of 213, they were eight-wheeled non-bogie carriage stock originally built by Brown Marshalls in 1883. No. 213 was built a year or two earlier by Ashbury Carriage and Wagon Company and was a similar vehicle. These vehicles were renumbered SW810-SW811-SW812-SW813 respectively in the London Transport numbering scheme, but were withdrawn and scrapped in 1941 when new sleet locomotives allocated to Neasden Depot became available.

As late as 1933, the winter before the formation of London Transport, three Sleet Wagons were constructed by the Underground Group and numbered SW211, 212 and 213, being box wagons designed to form an operating unit between two passenger or ballast motor cars. These vehicles were renumbered SW816 (SW213), SW817 (SW211) and SW818 (SW212) in 1936. At the west end of the Piccadilly Line there was a double wagon unit originally numbered SW191, but on the renumbering introduced in 1936 the two vehicles became SW814A and SW814B. This unit was, in fact, the first one to be replaced by a new Sleet Locomotive, being scrapped in 1939. Another Sleet Wagon allocated to the LER was SW192, which became SW815 in 1936.

All these special Sleet Wagons were scrapped between 1939 and 1942 as new Sleet Locomotives, constructed at Acton Works, became available. Prior to the decision to build these special Sleet Locomotives, however, an experiment was carried out in 1937 with a self-propelled Sleet Wagon using a bus engine and gearbox. This vehicle was numbered SL819 but did not in fact get beyond the experimental stage. Although, in principle, this might have been a satisfactory solution to the problem it was difficult to man in an emergency and, like many other vehicles used only intermittently, was not always available at the right time.

When tube lines were extended into the open — the Bakerloo in 1917 and the Hampstead to Edgware in 1925, followed by the Piccadilly in the early thirties — the difficulties with current collection in winter became acute because as a precaution against an electrical fusing incident, tube trains (unlike surface line rolling stock) were not permitted to have bus lines connecting all the collector shoes together. The first tube trains employed to extend the Bakerloo Line to Watford had to receive a special dispensation from the Board of Trade Railway Inspecting Officers to enable a bus line to be provided to connect up a positive collector shoe fitted to the first trailer car bogie adjacent to the Central London Railway motor cars which were used initially for the service, because there was insufficient clearance to fit an outside shoe on the trailing bogie on these motor cars. It was subsequently found necessary to provide sleet brushes on the motor cars themselves, and these Central London motor cars operating over the Watford line were in fact the first tube motor cars to be fitted with such brushes on the shoebeams, in front of the collector shoes. These brushes were let down at the stations where the trains came out of the tunnels and set up again by hand before the trains entered the tunnels to prevent excessive wear of the brushes, which were continually in contact with the current rail while lowered.

Subsequently, the Watford Joint Stock motor cars, when delivered, were equipped with two positive sleet brushes — one each side — and one negative brush. Adjustment of the position of the brushes was arranged at Queens Park on the northbound journey on the leading motor car and at Watford for the southbound journey, the brushes being lifted at Queens Park before the train entered the tunnel section. This arrangement was very expensive in manpower because car examiners had to be continuously on duty at the points where the position of the brushes was adjusted.

On the Hampstead Line after 1924, only a limited number of cars were fitted with sleet brushes, and these were identified by a white band bearing the letter 'S' in black on each corner of the leading end of the cant rail near the corner of the roof. These cars were usually concentrated on the Edgware service whenever the weather was inclement.

Two steam locomotives on the District Line were fitted with sleet brushes, and in addition 100 B Class District motor cars were equipped with such brushes. In 1932, following the extension of the Piccadilly Line on the open sections to Cockfosters in the north and beyond Hammersmith in the west, a number of motor cars on this line were also fitted with sleet brushes and labelled with the black 'S' in the same way as those operating on the Hampstead Line.

The 1935/40 Programme of extensions to the system proposed a very great increase in the open track working of tube trains. Some improvement in the weather forecasting was therefore sought in order to achieve an improvement in the current collection arrangements under rail icing conditions. Extremely exposed points of the railway were therefore selected to provide information concerning temperature and humidity which would give some information of the severity of the conditions. These positions proved to be too remote, so that the information given was more in the nature of history, enabling analysis of the condition to be made afterwards but failing to provide forecasts on which action could be taken.

Forecasts specific to the London Transport area commenced on 8th January 1948. Prior to this, the general weather forecasts available to the public had been used. When the special forecasts were received from the Meteorological Office from 1948 onwards the information was passed by the Railway Traffic Controllers to those sections requiring warning of trouble to come, to enable the preventive measures to be set in motion.

Unmanned weather recording stations were introduced by London Transport which enabled information to be provided from three sites spread across London. The first installation was at Queensbury on the Stanmore line which came into operation for the winters of 1950/51 and 1951/52 and then continuously from November 1952. A similar installation was introduced at Chorley Wood from July 1958 and then at Theydon Bois from the winter of 1959/60. This research programme was aimed at collecting information which would improve the de-icing arrangements and help the Meteorological Office to provide special forecasts about the possibility of icing of the conductor rails.

The forecasts now received from the Weather Centre between October and April are simplified into four categories — (1) No Risk, (2) Small Risk, (3) Risk and (4) Strong Risk.

When a forecast which indicated any significant degree of risk was received, the Railway Control Office alerted the Permanent Way Department so that they could prepare their precautionary arrangements, including the switching on of de-icing baths and other steps such as the cancellation of track work (necessitated by the fact that current remained switched on to facilitate the operation of sleet trains, point heaters and rail heating).

Clearing snow and ice physically from point mechanisms is necessary under certain conditions, but in recent years heating devices have been provided to minimise this. There are a number of different types of point heaters. In 1941, some installations, known at that time as 'Snow Melters' were fitted at vulnerable positions over the system. They consisted of eight tubular heaters at each location, four on each side of the track, lying on the ballast between the sleepers and below the running rails. The eight heaters, connected in series, were charged from the traction supply when switched on.

In 1942, an improved type of heater was introduced using oil electrically heated and thermostatically controlled, circulating round vulnerable track points. Electrical heaters can be switched on and off by remote control. In some depot locations where attention can be given on the spot, gas point heaters have been provided but these require to be lit and turned off locally when not required and therefore need some manual attention. Difficulties can also arise should a derailment occur adjacent to gas point heaters.

When signal boxes were located near point heaters and signalling installations, observation of conditions was almost constant and the effect of cold conditions could be overcome or help sought. With the introduction of automation and remote control it is more difficult to combat ice and snow because predictions are required at long range and fewer pairs of hands are available to deal physically with the problems at the site.

Several District Line B type cars were earmarked for conversion into self-propelled sleet wagons powered by petrol engines but this idea was later abandoned. However, when the old Central London motor cars were made available by the 1935/40 Programme of stock replacement, it was decided to use them to provide a number of sleet locomotives. Each sleet locomotive was formed from two old Central London motor cars which had been cut behind the motor bogie and joined back to back by the insertion of a new body piece similar to the way L10, the Acton Yard shunting locomotive, had been made.

It was originally intended that 20 sleet locomotives would be built and 40 Central London motor cars of 1903/4 vintage were earmarked for conversion. The work began at Acton Works in 1938 and was completed by 1941, but by this time the number of sleet locomotives required had been reduced to 18. The original plan had been to provide 13 for the existing open sections of electrified track plus seven more for the proposed Northern and Central Line extensions under the 1935/40 Programme. The locomotives were numbered ESL100 to ESL117 and the first went into trial service on 22nd December 1938.

The first design consisted of a locomotive 38 feet long with only one de-icing bogie. Unfortunately this length of locomotive ran into gapping difficulties on the current rails and the bulk conversion arranged for the sleet locomotives to be 50 feet long with two de-icing bogies.

At first the traction equipment already installed was used including the GE66 traction motors. In later years during overhauls, the traction control equipment was changed as more modern equipment became available, but unfortunately bogie clearance problems made it very difficult to replace the GE66 type motor. This type of motor, designed about the turn of the century, was not fitted with interpoles and among other problems such motors had a tendency to flash over. As it was desirable in any case that the locomotives when working, should operate at a slow speed in order to deposit anti-freeze solution properly, it was arranged that they would not operate beyond series, so that one of the critical flash-over conditions, the change from

ESL111, completed in 1940 at Acton Works from Central London cars 3956 and 3959. This locomotive was withdrawn in 1982.

series to parallel, was eliminated. The vehicles were of course double equipped, having one set of equipment at each end and each controlling two traction motors. As sleet locomotives would not be required to stop in stations the speed limitation of remaining with each pair of motors in series would not be inhibiting to the service apart from long runs, like that between Hammersmith and Acton Town, unless some other problems arose.

Under the new centre portion of the locomotive, two non load-bearing trailer bogies were provided, on to which was fitted de-icing gear. This equipment consisted of ice cutters, sleet brushes and anti-freeze spray nozzles. The ice cutters consisted of rotating hard-steel ridged rollers which were pressed down by a compressed air cylinder to make contact with the current rail. The sleet brushes, similar to those which have been used before on many vehicles, had metal prongs. A brush was placed on either side of the cutter so that sweeping was carried out both before and after cutting in either direction.

When the Sleet Locomotives were first operated it was necessary to provide the driver with a mate to operate the valves, selecting the side on which the positive rail was located, as these changed from side to side. However, in 1955, the operation of the dispensing equipment for the de-icing fluid was made automatic, under the control of pneumatic valves which were activated by a shoe detecting device which sensed the positive rail. When the detecting shoe dropped below rail level, it activated a contact which de-energised the spray control valve on that side. The fluid was also controlled when the brakes were applied, which in any case was a straight pneumatic application on the Westinghouse principle, so that it was not difficult to link into the pneumatic control of the dispensing equipment.

The automatic control was achieved by the use of electro-pneumatic valves, the current being obtained from two sets of 50-volt batteries charged from the 600-volt supply. The air supply was obtained from the main reservoir and reduced to 30psi (by a reducing valve) to operate the control valves which activated the cutters, sleet brushes and de-icing fluid dispenser nozzles.

The tank containing the de-icing fluid was situated in the central part of the locomotives, to which loading access was provided on either side by means of a sliding door.

In 1962 some further modifications were made to the locomotives, including the provision of more modern control equipments which became available following the scrapping of the T stock. These equipments were electro-pneumatic in operation and not themselves dependent on collecting power from the current rails, as the previous equipments had been. Current for control was provided by the battery. The original equipments had been electro-magnetic and required 600-volt control circuits for operation, so that when the sleet locomotives themselves were having current rail problems the traction control was also in difficulty. At the same time as the newer control equipments were fitted the opportunity was taken to replace the galvanised iron piping (which corroded from the de-icing fluid) with plastic piping which overcame the blockage problems. When the locomotives had been originally constructed, plastic piping was not available. ESL108 was the first locomotive to be treated and the others followed as and when they could be passed through Acton Works.

ESL103 was the first sleet locomotive to be scrapped. It suffered collision damage in May 1948 and was sent to Acton Works for repair. However, these repairs were considered to be too extensive to permit economical rebuilding and the vehicle was scrapped in 1954.

When the Metropolitan Line was electrified beyond Rickmansworth in 1961, it was decided to provide an additional sleet locomotive. T stock cars were available, so two of them, 2758 and 2749, were retained and converted into a double sleet locomotive with the two vehicles being permanently coupled together. They were renumbered ESL118A and ESL118B, but were always operated together. The equipment was, of course, electro-pneumatic, of the same type as that salvaged from other T stock vehicles to fit to the older sleet locomotives. The dispensing equipment was fitted to the existing inner motor bogies.

In practice the sleet locomotives were in the nature of a cure after the cold weather had begun to take its toll but positive efforts were necessary to try to prevent the formation of ice rather than cure its effects.

In 1944 a de-icing bath which coated the underside of the collector shoe with de-icing fluid was produced and inserted in the current rail. A large scale experiment was put in hand on the Stanmore line which by the end of 1945 had been fully provided with this equipment.

In 1947 it was decided to install conductor rail de-icing baths at vulnerable places over most of the system. It was visualised that as soon as inclement weather was forecast, the baths would become operative and distribute the fluid over the rails. However, after baths were installed, some difficulties arose because of splashing of the shoebeams with de-icing fluid, causing severe flashovers and arcing and leading to serious fusing incidents. Each bath contained a rubber or plastic roller which transferred the fluid from the tank part underneath on to the underside of the collector shoe, which then spread the fluid along the conductor rail. When this was accomplished at high speed the roller continued to rotate after the passage of the shoe, causing a spray of the de-icing liquid which was then deposited on the rolling stock. The use of the baths was then restricted to really inclement weather so that they were therefore not very much more effective than the sleet locomotives and then only on the piece of track adjacent to the bath. The de-icing baths did not then eliminate the need for sleet locomotives, although they did reduce the number of times they were required to operate.

Having found that de-icing baths alone would not meet the needs of winter conditions, a further development by LT came in 1957 with what was described as a sleet tender. This was a small four-wheeled vehicle, almost going back to the original pre-war sleet wagon, but this time the idea was to attach it to the front of a passenger train so that it could be operated by a normal service crew and not necessarily those allocated for sleet locomotive duties, who have to be specially trained. The sleet tender gave an unobstructed view forward for the driver, yet provided the de-icing application.

Side view of sleet tender for pushing in front of passenger train, showing positive rail locating roller for dispensing de-icing fluid, sleet brushes and ice crusher together with their individual pneumatic cylinders.

Sleet tender attached to passenger train. Two of these were built at Acton in 1957 and were used on the Piccadilly Line. They were nicknamed 'prams' by the trainmen.

Two prototype tenders were completed at Acton Works in 1957 and were based at Northfields Depot for testing on the Piccadilly Line with the idea that, if successful, they would take over from the specialised sleet locomotives that at this time still had their original obsolete equipment, which was in need of replacement.

The tenders, consisting of a specially constructed four-wheel bogie fitted with the de-icing equipment similar to that provided on the sleet locomotives and detecting gear to determine which side the positive rail was to be found, were fitted with a spring-applied brake, which was released when air pressure was applied by attaching the vehicle to a train. This arrangement ensured that if the tender broke away from its parent train, the brake would be applied. The arrangement proposed was that a tender would be placed at both ends of a normal passenger formation so that one tender would be out of use at the trailing end, while the one at the leading end would be operative. Two inter-connected tanks, containing 75 gallons, were mounted on top of the bogie frame for supplying the de-icing fluid, which was dispensed through the sprays by an axle-driven pump. This pump could be disengaged if the dispensing of fluid was not required. The de-icing fluid flow was controlled by mechanically operated cut-off valves located on each side, activated by a lever carrying a roller which rode on the positive rail. When this roller dropped below a low limit, the spray was cut off.

While the idea was an attempt to obtain a reasonable compromise between having special locomotives and every train fitted with its own de-icing equipment, difficulties arose with the signalling because this had been developed with very tight limits to the positioning of blockjoints operating the trainstops. Adopting the sleet tender arrangement would have necessitated expensive alterations to the signalling, including provision of longer train berths.

In 1962, an experiment tried a long time ago was resurrected and tried again to combat this problem of icing of current rails. This consisted of passing a continuous current through the rails sufficient to raise their temperature. As long ago as 1908, the Hounslow Line, then part of the District Railway, had the rails heated by Acton Town sub-station feeding the current rails by providing a short circuit applied at the Hounslow end of the tracks. This arrangement was re-introduced in 1962 on the section between Croxleyhall and Chorleywood sub-stations. Something like 4000 amperes, equivalent to a power consumption of 2400Kw, was required to raise the temperature to about 70°F. Such an arrangement cannot of course be adopted when trains are running, but can be used during the hours of night to try to keep the rails clear for the service in the morning. Areas which can be heated by this short circuit method have signs which display the legend 'heated conductor rails over this section during winter months'. Other sections on the Piccadilly and Central Lines as well as the Metropolitan Line have been treated in this fashion.

Experiments were carried out on behalf of London Transport in the Vickers Armstrong cold chamber laboratory at Weybridge in 1962, to see if there was any possible way of improving the de-icing precautions on the current rails. One arrangement which showed considerable promise was the utilisation of a compressed air jet at high pressure, associated with a rotating scraper, but the advantage was subsequently found to be only marginally better than the scrapers and brushes provided on the sleet locomotives and very expensive to maintain.

The operation of sleet locomotives required the provision of special crewing arrangements or the cancellation of passenger trains to provide the sleet train working, so that following the failure of the de-icing tender developed in 1957, it was decided to equip a certain percentage of the passenger rolling stock with in-built de-icing equipment. Certain trailer cars of 1959/62 Tube Stock for working on the Central and Piccadilly Lines were equipped with tanks under the floor to contain de-icing fluid and were provided with a beam similar to a shoebeam, mounted on the trucks and carrying de-icing sprays. The cars equipped with this equipment had the letter 'D' placed under the car number. A total of 30 × four-car units was provided on the Piccadilly Line, the trailer cars concerned being numbered between 2100 and 2216. These units were subsequently transferred to the Northern Line during 1978/79. On the Central Line, trailer cars having a number ending in '6' between 2406 and 2646 were converted and this provided 25 × four-car units for operation on the main part of the Line. In addition, the units working the shuttle service between Hainault and Woodford were all fitted with de-icing equipment on one of the two Pre-1938 Tube Stock cars, originally forming part of the four-car units. Subsequently three of these units were modified at Acton Works, replacing the two Pre-1938 Tube Stock cars in each unit by one 1938 Tube Stock trailer car, making each into a three-car set. The 1938 Tube Stock trailers however, were fitted with de-icing equipment, the conversion beginning in 1977.

A number of COP stock trailer cars in three-car units were also converted to carry de-icing equipment for operation on the District Line, with special reference to the Edgware Road to Putney Bridge and Wimbledon sections. Seven cars were so equipped — 013080, 013090, 013091, 013144, 013172, 013272 and 014070, the numbers being chosen virtually at random as they became available for the work to be executed.

85

Special timetable workings were then introduced on each of these lines to ensure that during winter weather a coverage of de-icing fluid once every two or three hours would be possible over each track by arranging that trailer cars dispensing the fluid were placed in appropriate trains. On the Piccadilly Line the four-car unit was always at one end of the seven-car train so that in the westbound direction the de-icing fluid tended to be wiped off by the three-car unit behind, while in the eastbound direction the de-icing protection was at the back of the train. On the Central Line, the de-icing unit could be at either end of the train since the eight-car formation is made up of two four-car units and it was wasteful to have two units on a train with de-icing equipment. In very severe weather over a continuous period the provision of de-icing trailers was less than adequate because of the difficulty of having them continuously in the right place, always topped up with fluid and the equipment working correctly. Continuous severe weather occurs so rarely in the English climate, especially in the London area, that over-provision of facilities is considered to be more wasteful than the occasional hiatus caused by under-provision.

When the 1972 MkI stock was delivered, there was no provision for de-icing trailers so the Northern Line relied upon current rail baths. However, on the 1972 MkII stock, which was provided originally for eventual operation on the Jubilee Line, 12 four-car units with trailer cars 4352 to 4363 were fitted with de-icing equipment. These cars went into service first on the Northern Line before being ultimately transferred to the Jubilee Line, by which time the Northern Line was provided with the 1959 Tube Stock transferred from the Piccadilly Line to continue the de-icing.

The 1973 Tube Stock for the Piccadilly Line, replacing the 1959 Tube Stock on this line, was also provided with de-icing trailers, 25 in number on even numbered trailer cars from 604 to 652 so that these were also always at the west end of the train. The 1973 Tube Stock enabled the 1959 Tube Stock to be transferred to the Northern Line and the 1972 MkII to the Jubilee Line, which acquired the open sections of the Bakerloo Line from Finchley Road to Stanmore.

The A stock on the Metropolitan Line, probably the most vulnerable to winter conditions, was in fact the first to have de-icing equipment fitted to some cars. Eighteen units, with even-numbered trailers 6088 to 6122, were modified to take the de-icing equipment. As built, the A stock was formed into four-car reversible units and made up into eight-car trains by coupling two units together so that the position of the de-icing trailer could not be predicted in any formation.

When the C69 Stock was constructed, it was arranged that 14 of the two-car units should be equipped with de-icing equipment and trailer cars 6543 to 6556 were so fitted.

The new District Line rolling stock, the D stock, is made up with three-car units. The de-icing equipment has been fitted to 25 of the 'A' end units of D stock, so that the dispensing of fluid will always be at the end leading when the trains are going westbound and trailing when travelling eastbound.

All lines which operate open sections now have de-icing fluid dispensing trains, and by August 1985 there were no sleet locomotives left in active service, the last one having been used only for shunting duties.

Another problem akin to de-icing is the difficulty which arises in the autumn when the leaves are falling, because certain conditions of humidity, together with the type and quantity of leaves, provide a condition on the track which reduces adhesion. Loss of adhesion produces two detrimental conditions; wheels 'pick up' during braking and lock, and wheels spin during acceleration.

In the Chilterns on the Metropolitan Line between Northwood Hills and Amersham there is a serious problem due to the loss of adhesion in the autumn caused by this combination of falling leaves and humidity. The British Railways diesel trains suffer from wheel slip because they rely upon a small number of motor bogies to provide the motive power, while London Transport trains with high braking rates suffer from wheel pick up on braking, producing flatted wheels.

In 1972, ESL100 and ESL112 were modified for additional duties, being fitted with brushes to clean running rails, for use during the autumn, to clear the rails of leaves. ESL100 was also fitted with equipment to enable the running rails to be sprayed with water to assist in this cleaning process.

Reservoirs were mounted in the body of the locomotive which could be filled with water or any adhesion-improving fluid, of which a number were tried. Main line air pressure forced the fluid through nozzles mounted on the D end of the sleet locomotive. Retractable brushes for sweeping the running rails were also fitted to special beams placed on the bogies and were so arranged that they did not sweep off the deposition of fluid. After a number of detailed experiments no suitable fluid was found and the locomotive was then confined to sweeping only.

In 1978 further experiments were arranged, this time with a special train made up to deal with the falling leaves. The original formation consisted of 'Sarah Siddons' (the remaining Metropolitan Locomotive No. 12) together with a brake van and a flat car equipped with high pressure jets coupled to the two T stock sleet locomotives ESL118A and ESL118B. The actual make up was ESL118A-ESL118B-B558-F311-Loco No. 12; F311 contained two 2,000 gallon water tanks and pumping equipment provided by a Merlin bus engine. The sleet locomotives were replaced by ballast motor L149 in 1979. These trains worked out of Neasden with different formations from time to time.

Troubles were also experienced on the South Harrow branch of the Piccadilly Line and the rail grinding unit was used for leaf-cleaning purposes.

The use of high pressure water was found to be the most efficacious and in 1980 F311 was formed into a unit between ESL118A and ESL118B for leaf-clearing duty. Water was sprayed on to the running rails at high pressure, the controls being provided in the 'luggage' end of ESL118A. Also provided on this unit was a means of depositing an adhesion-improving compound which has been found to work. It consists of sand and either chromium or stainless steel particles suspended in a gel. The metal particles are to ensure track circuit operation. This was quite successful but the whole unit (ESL118A-F311-ESL118B) has become too old to use frequently and has been replaced by a 'Unimog' leaf clearing road/rail machine which picks up leaves to try to prevent the problem occurring.

Special leaf clearing train with 'Sarah Siddons' trailing and 1938 stock ballast motors leading at Amersham. This was the beginning of a long series of trials which searched for a solution to the leaf-fall problem on the Underground.

Leaf-clearing flat wagon between ESL118A and ESL118B, another variation of the trains used to deal with the problem. ESL118A and 118B are former T stock vehicles built in 1933 and converted in 1961 after replacement on the Metropolitan Line by A stock.

LT Service Stock List

LT STEAM LOCOS

LT No.	Original No.	Class	Origin & Date	Type	Date Acquired	Builder	Scrapped	Notes
L30			DIST .31	0-6-0 T		Hunslet Engine Co	30.7.64	1
L31			DIST .31	0-6-0 T		Hunslet Engine Co	30.7.64	1
L34	L33X		LER .22	0-4-2 ST		Kerr Stuart	31.3.49	2
L44	1	E	MET .1898	0-4-4 T		Neasden Works	20.3.64	3, 18
L45	23	A	MET .1866	4-4-0 T		Beyer Peacock	3.6.48	4, 18
L46	77	E	MET .1896	0-4-4 T		Neasden Works	15.2.63	5, 18
L47	80	E	MET .00	0-4-4 T		Hawthorn Leslie	21.7.41	17, 18
L48	81	E	MET 1.01	0-4-4 T		Hawthorn Leslie	30.7.64	1, 18
L49	90	F	MET .01	0-6-2 T		Yorkshire Eng Co	24.9.57	6, 18
L50	91	F	MET .01	0-6-2 T		Yorkshire Eng Co	6.4.59	7, 18
L51	92	F	MET .01	0-6-2 T		Yorkshire Eng Co	4.7.57	8, 18
L52	93	F	MET 5.01	0-6-2 T		Yorkshire Eng Co	30.7.64	1, 18
L53	101	B	MET 3.1897	0-6-0 ST		Peckett & Sons	3.8.60	9, 18
L54	102	B	MET 11.1899	0-6-0 ST		Peckett & Sons	7.3.62	10, 18
L89	5775		GWR 29	0-6-0 PT	8.8.63	GWR	20.1.70	11
L90	7711		GWR 6.30	0-6-0 PT	7.10.56	Kerr Stuart	29.9.61	12
L90	7760		GWR 1.31	0-6-0 PT	14.11.61	North British	3.9.71	16
L91	5752		GWR 4.29	0-6-0 PT	25.2.57	GWR	18.11.60	12
L91	5757		GWR 5.29	0-6-0 PT	18.11.60	GWR	29.1.70	13
L92	5786		GWR 1.30	0-6-0 PT	20.4.58	GWR	3.10.69	14
L93	7779		GWR 11.30	0-6-0 PT	5.10.58	Armstrong Whitworth	8.9.68	15
L94	7752		GWR 11.30	0-6-0 PT	1.11.59	North British	8.6.71	16
L95	5764		GWR 7.29	0-6-0 PT	22.5.60	GWR	19.6.71	17
L96	7741		GWR 2.30	0-6-0 PT	14.11.61	North British	21.9.67	15
L97	7749		GWR 3.30	0-6-0 PT	11.8.62	North British	29.1.70	7
L98	7739		GWR 2.30	0-6-0 PT	4.12.62	North British	29.1.70	7
L99	7715		GWR 2.30	0-6-0 PT	24.6.63	Kerr Stuart	1.1.70	3

NOTES
1 Cut up at Neasden by Lacmots Ltd.
2 Originally named 'BRAZIL', withdrawn /35, reinstated /37.
3 Sold to London Railway Preservation Society, Dunmow, to Quainton Road.
4 Preserved by LT at Clapham, Syon Park and now LT Museum, at Covent Garden.
5 Cut up at Neasden by Parry Ltd.
6 Sold to R. Adair.
7 Cut up at Neasden by SBD, Chesterfield.
8 Sold to Holinter, removed by road (collision Neasden 29.9.56).
9 Cut up at Neasden by Cohens.
10 Cut up at Neasden by Cox & Danks.
11 Preserved by K & WVR, in LT Livery.
12 Returned to BR (WR).
13 Originally numbered L96; renumbered in 1961.
14 Sold to Worcester Loco Preservation Society, Hereford.
15 Cut up at Neasden by Cashmores.
16 Sold to Standard Gauge Steam Trust, Tyseley, West Midlands.
17 Sold to Severn Valley Railway, Bridgnorth.
18 Transferred to Service Stock 1.11.37, ex Met Rly.

LT ELECTRIC LOCOS

METROPOLITAN RAILWAY

No.	Origin	Named	Became Shunting Locos	Scrapped	Notes
1	1922/3 MV	John Lyon	29.1.62 Neasden	23.8.74	1
2	1922/3 MV	Oliver Cromwell		8.3.62	2, 3
3	1922/3 MV	Sir Ralph Verney	29.1.62 Ruislip	30.5.65	4
4	1922/3 MV	Lord Byron		22.1.62	5
5	1922/3 MV	John Hampden	29.1.62 Acton	9.3.73	6
6	1922/3 MV	William Penn		22.1.62	5
7	1922/3 MV	Edmund Burke		8.3.62	3
8	1922/3 MV	Sherlock Holmes		22.1.62	5
9	1922/3 MV	John Milton	23.3.50 Ealing	2.3.62	5
10	1922/3 MV	William Ewart Gladstone		22.1.62	5, 7
11	1922/3 MV	George Romney		22.1.62	5
12	1922/3 MV	Sarah Siddons	29.1.62 Ealing		8
13	1922/3 MV	Dick Whittington		22.1.62	5
14	1922/3 MV	Benjamin Disraeli		7.3.62	5, 17
15	1922/3 MV	Wembley 1924		18.9.51	9
16	1922/3 MV	Oliver Goldsmith		8.3.62	3, 13
17	1922/3 MV	Florence Nightingale		11.10.43	14
18	1922/3 MV	Michael Faraday		8.3.62	3
19	1922/3 MV	John Wycliffe		12.3.48	10, 15
20	1922/3 MV	Sir Christopher Wren		26.4.54	11, 16
21	1905 MAR			4.3.48	12

DISTRICT RAILWAY

LER No.	Origin	Original No.	Converted to	Scrapped	Note
L1	1905 MAR	8A		31.10.39	18
L2	1905 MAR	2A		1.7.38	
L3	1905 MAR	3A		17.11.39	
L4	1905 MAR	4A		17.11.39	
L5	1905 MAR	5A		16.10.39	
L6	1905 MAR	6A		16.10.39	
L7	1905 MAR	7A		1.7.38	
L8	1909 Renshaw	19A	Electric 3.24	25.9.69	19
L9	1909 Renshaw	20A	Electric 2.24	25.9.69	19

NOTES

1 Cut up at Neasden by Birds.
2 Re-named 'Thomas Lord'.
3 To BR(LMR) Mitre Bridge, thence Rugby.
4 Cut up at Ruislip by Cashmores.
5 Neasden to T.W. Ward, Killamarsh, for scrap.
6 Preserved by LT at Syon Park, now Covent Garden.
7 Re-named W.E. Gladstone.
8 Exhibited at Shildon 1975. LPTB livery 5/82.
9 Exhibited at Wembley Exhibition, 1925, and named 'Wembley 1924'.
10 Collision Northwood 31.12.45.
11 Collision Rickmansworth 31.5.52, cut up at Acton by Cohens.
12 Body from Met No.1 in 1921; original scrapped. Re-numbered L33 on 28.2.36.
13 Allocated to GN & C from late 1934 to 1936.
14 Prototype Loco conversion, Neasden 1921, first to be named 3.10.27.
15 First in LPTB livery.
16 First in grey livery, nameplates removed.
17 First in post-war LT livery.
18 Later re-numbered 1A.
19 Originally battery loco. Cut up at Ealing Common by T.W. Ward.

EX-GATE STOCK SERVICE LOCOS

Final No.	Original No.	Origin		Renumbered		Converted to			Renumbered		Scrapped	Notes
L10	1 & 3	5.07	ACF	3 to 2	8.26	Acton Shunter	L10	6.30			30.9.78	1
L11	39	11.07	Hungarian	118	9.26	Battery	L12	7.29	L11	3.11.36	21.8.40	
L12	34	12.06	Hungarian	113	9.26	Battery	L11	7.29	L12	3.11.36	21.8.40	
L13	42	12.07	Hungarian	121	9.26	Ballast	L13	7.29			5.10.55	3
L14	41	11.07	Hungarian	120	9.26	Ballast	L14	7.29			14.9.54	2
L15	44	12.07	Hungarian	123	9.26	Ballast	L15	7.29			9.9.55	3
L16	51	3.09	Hungarian	128	9.26	Ballast	L16	7.29			28.2.61	4
L17	50	5.07	Hungarian	127	9.26	Ballast	L17	7.29			8.9.55	3
L18	53	2.07	Hungarian	130	9.26	Ballast	L18	7.29			5.10.55	3
L19	71	11.07	Hungarian	137	9.26	Ballast	L19	7.29			8.9.55	3
L20	57	3.09	Hungarian	134	9.26	Ballast	L20	7.29			19.9.55	3
L21	12	.00	GEC				L21	6.32	30.6.42			
L22	54	.01	CLR	201	.03	Battery	L22	.30			22.12.36	5
L23	81	.01	CLR	202	.03	Battery	L23	.31			3.4.37	5
L24	29	11.06	French	497	1.26	Ballast	L25	14.6.30	L24	28.10.36	21.10.52	3
L25	2	11.06	French	480	1.26	Ballast	L24	17.7.30	L25	28.10.36	27.9.52	3
L26	7	2.06	French	483	1.26	Ballast	L27	17.7.30	L26	28.10.36	12.7.54	2
L27	6	11.06	French	482	1.26	Ballast	L26	28.6.30	L27	28.10.36	8.9.54	2
L28	11	11.06	French	485	1.26	Ballast	L29	17.7.30	L28	28.10.36	27.9.55	3
L29	10	11.06	French	484	1.26	Ballast	L28	17.7.30	L29	28.10.36	15.7.54	2
L32	14	3.06	ACF	66	12.26	Battery	L32	3.32			6.3.48	

NOTES
1 Cut up at Acton by Cashmores.
2 Cut up at Ruislip by Cohens.
3 Cut up at Ruislip by SBD, Chesterfield.
4 Cut up at Ruislip by Parry. Gate End preserved by LT at Clapham then Syon Park, now Covent Garden.
5 Originally CLR loco-hauled trailers, to motors in 1902. Re-numbered 201/2 in 1903.

LT SERVICE LOCOS

LT No.	Original No.	Origin	Type	Converted	Delivered	Scrapped
L11	3080/3109	1931 MCW	Acton Works Shunter	19.6.64		
L13A	10130	1938 MCW	Acton Works Shunter	3.74		
L13B	11130	1938 MCW	Acton Works Shunter	3.74		
L14A	10011	1935 MCW	Acton Works Shunter	8.70		16.2.75
L14B	11011	1935 MCW	Acton Works Shunter	8.70		16.2.75
L15		1969 MCW	Battery		23.4.70	
L16		1969 MCW	Battery		21.5.70	
L17		1969 MCW	Battery		12.6.70	
L18		1969 MCW	Battery		29.6.70	
L19		1969 MCW	Battery		27.7.70	
L20		1964 MCW	Battery		8.12.64	
L21		1964 MCW	Battery		19.12.64	
L22		1964 MCW	Battery		13.1.65	
L23		1964 MCW	Battery		13.1.65	
L24		1964 MCW	Battery		28.1.65	
L25		1964 MCW	Battery		13.3.65	
L26		1964 MCW	Battery		1.4.65	
L27		1964 MCW	Battery		22.4.65	
L28		1964 MCW	Battery		7.5.65	
L29		1964 MCW	Battery		21.5.65	
L30		1964 MCW	Battery		11.6.65	
L31		1964 MCW	Battery		25.6.65	
L32		1964 MCW	Battery		23.7.65	
*L33	L76	1962 Acton	Battery	31.7.62		
L35		1938 GRCW	Battery		25.2.38	
L36		1938 GRCW	Battery		4.3.38	
L37		1938 GRCW	Battery		11.3.38	
L38		1938 GRCW	Battery		18.3.38	
L39		1938 GRCW	Battery		29.3.38	
L40		1938 GRCW	Battery		12.4.38	
L41		1938 GRCW	Battery		29.11.37	16.9.78
L42		1938 GRCW	Battery		20.12.37	16.9.78
L43		1938 GRCW	Battery		25.1.38	17.1.80
L44		1973 BREL	Battery		22.1.74	
L45		1973 BREL	Battery		12.2.74	
L46		1973 BREL	Battery		26.2.74	

*Renumbered L33 in January 1974.

LT No.	Origins				Type	Converted	Delivered	Scrapped
L47	1973 BREL Doncaster				Battery		2.4.74	
L48	1973 BREL Doncaster				Battery		2.4.74	
L49	1973 BREL Doncaster				Battery		23.4.74	
L50	1973 BREL Doncaster				Battery		14.5.74	
L51	1973 BREL Doncaster				Battery		4.6.74	
L52	1973 BREL Doncaster				Battery		25.6.74	
L53	1973 BREL Doncaster				Battery		23.7.74	
L54	1973 BREL Doncaster				Battery		28.8.74	
L55	1951 Pickering				Battery		8.1.51	
L56	1951 Pickering				Battery		20.3.51	
L57	1951 Pickering				Battery		29.5.51	
L58	1951 Pickering				Battery		17.7.51	
L59	1951 Pickering				Battery		19.9.51	
L60	1951 Pickering				Battery		19.11.51	
L61	1951 Pickering				Battery		30.4.52	
L62	1985 MCW				Battery		6.9.85	
L63	1985 MCW				Battery		4.10.85	
L64	1985 MCW				Battery		25.10.85	
L65	1985 MCW				Battery		29.11.85	
L66	1985 MCW				Battery		13.12.85	
L67	1985 MCW				Battery		28.2.86	
L62	1923 CL	512	3452	6.34	Ballast	2.9.54		5.10.73
L63	1923 CL	523	3463	12.34	Ballast	15.7.54		25.9.78
L64	1923 MCW	560	3500	9.33	Ballast	2.3.55		27.9.78
L65	1923 CL	513	3453	9.34	Ballast	19.8.54		20.5.78
L66	1923 CL	536	3476	6.35	Ballast	18.3.54		6.3.74
L67	1923 MCW	561	3501	5.34	Ballast	19.1.55		31.10.73
L68	1923 MCW	554	3494	3.35	Ballast	12.10.54		19.9.78
L69	1923 MCW	565	3505	11.34	Ballast	21.9.54		5.10.73
L70	1923 MCW	556	3496	4.35	Ballast	15.7.54		13.9.75
L71	1923 MCW	567	3507	12.34	Ballast	2.4.54		27.9.78
L72	1923 MCW	558	3498	8.34	Ballast	21.9.54		23.6.64
L72	1927 MCW	326	3376	3.34	Ballast	13.6.64		25.6.71
L73	1923 MCW	573	3513	11.33	Ballast	18.5.54		22.8.67
L74	1923 MCW	566	3506	4.33	Ballast	18.5.54		22.9.78
L75	1923 MCW	577	3517	7.35	Ballast	28.10.54		21.9.78
L77	1931 MCW		3183		Ballast	3.11.67		20.9.78

No.	Origins	Type	Delivered
DL81	1968 Thomas Hill (Rotherham)	0-6-0 Diesel	12.3.71
DL82	1967 Thomas Hill (Rotherham)	0-6-0 Diesel	25.5.71
DL83	1967 Thomas Hill (Rotherham)	0-6-0 Diesel	7.6.71

LT No.	Origins		Re-No.		Converted	Type	Scrapped	Notes
L126	1938 GRCW (Q38)	4416			3.72	Pilot		2
L127	1938 GRCW (Q38)	4417			3.72	Pilot		2
L128	1938 GRCW (Q38)	4418			3.72	Pilot	25.1.83	2
L129	1938 GRCW (Q38)	4419			3.72	Pilot	25.1.83	2
L130	1934 MCW	3690			25.9.67	Pilot		3
L131	1934 MCW	3693			18.9.67	Pilot		3
	1931 MCW	3138	3338	7.65		Pilot	16.7.70	1, 3
	1934 MCW	3707				Pilot	16.7.70	1, 3
L132	1960 Cravens	3901			.87	TRC Pilot		6
L133	1960 Cravens	3905			.87	TRC Pilot		6
L134	1927 MCW	320	3370	6.34	11.7.68	Pilot		3
L135	1934 MCW	3701			11.7.68	Pilot		3
	1927 MCW	312	3380	12.33		Pilot	28.6.71	1, 3
	1931 MCW	3073	3273	9.65		Pilot		1, 3,
L140	1938 MCW	10088			5.73	Ballast	24.1.80	5
L140	1938 MCW	10182			9.80	Ballast		
L141	1938 MCW	11067			6.73	Ballast		
L142	1938 MCW	10021			12.73	Ballast		
L143	1938 MCW	10065			12.73	Ballast		
L144	1938 MCW	10257			12.75	Ballast		
L145	1938 MCW	11027			12.75	Ballast		
L146	1938 MCW	10034			9.76	Ballast		
L147	1938 MCW	11034			9.76	Ballast		
L148	1938 MCW	10022			6.77	Ballast		
L149	1938 MCW	11104			8.77	Ballast		
L150	1938 MCW	90327	10327	1.53	7.78	Ballast		7
L151	1938 MCW	91327	11327	1.53	7.78	Ballast		7
L152	1938 MCW	10266			5.78	Ballast		
L153	1938 MCW	11266			5.78	Ballast		
L154	1938 MCW	10141			9.78	Ballast		
L155	1938 MCW	11141			9.78	Ballast	22.11.85	
TCC1	1938 MCW	10226			.76			
TCC2	1976 Acton							
TCC3	1976 Acton							
TCC4	1976 Acton							
TCC5	1938 MCW	10087			.76			

Tunnel Cleaner (TCC2/3/4 are trailers)

NOTES
1 Intended Renumbering L132/3 & 136/7.
2 Pilots from 9.71
3 Pilots from 2.67
4 To Isle of Wight on 20.3.71
5 Became L140 in June 1973; first numbered L84.
6 Converted by BREL Derby into Track Recording Car Pilots.
7 Weed Killing Ballast Motors

TAMPING MACHINES

No.	Delivered	Type		Disposal
PBT 760	9.59	Plasser VKR 04	26.5.70	Scrapped
PBT 761	5.4.67	VKR 05	11.84	Scrapped
PBT 762	5.4.67	VKR 05	26.10.84	To Southern Steam Trust, Swanage
PBT 763	5.4.67	VKR 05	11.84	Scrapped
PTL 764	73	AL 250	25.1.85	To Severn Valley Railway
SC 765	75	PLM 07275		
TMM 771	4.80	PU 0716		
TMM 772	4.80	PU 0716		
TMM 773	4.80	PU 0716		

CRANES

LT No.	Type	Origin & Date	Builder			Scrapped	Note
C 600	5 Ton	1895 Hand Crane	Jessop & Appleby	Ex-DR	C181	18.5.53	
C 601	5 Ton	1900 Trav. Crane	CLR	Ex-CLR	C185	1.5.37	
C 602	5 Ton	1904 Trav. Crane	Grafton Engineering Co	Ex-DR	C182	7.12.70	
C 603	5 Ton	1907 Trav. Crane	Taylor & Hubbard	Ex-LER	C184	15.1.65	
C 604	50 Ton	1925 Trav. Crane	Cowan & Sheldon	Ex-MR	C178	1.6.65	
C 605	5 Ton	1925 Trav. Crane	Grafton Engineering Co	Ex-DR	C187	4.83	
C 606	30 Ton	1931 Trav. Crane	Ransome & Rapier	Ex-DR	C188	15.2.86	1
C 607	10 Ton	1931 Trav. Crane	Ransome & Rapier	Ex-DR	C189	18.10.62	
C 608	5 Ton	1936 Steam Crane	Booth			1.1.58	4
C 609	5 Ton	1937 Steam Crane	Taylor & Hubbard			14.3.68	4
C 610	5 Ton	1937 Steam Crane	Grafton Engineering Co			27.2.73	4
C 611	5 Ton	1937 Steam Crane	Thomas Smith & Sons			27.2.73	4
C 612	3 Ton	1938 Steam Crane	Thomas Smith & Sons			15.10.54	
C 613	5 Ton	1938 Steam Crane	Grafton Engineering Co			7.12.70	
C 614	3 Ton	1938 Steam Crane	Thomas Smith & Sons			27.2.73	4
C 615	3 Ton	1904 Steam Crane	H.J. Coles Ltd	Ex-PW New Works 3.5.39		4.11.59	
C 616	5 Ton	1939 Steam Crane	Butler & Co			13.7.81	5
DEC 617	6 Ton	1955 Diesel Electric	Taylor & Hubbard				
DEC 618	6 Ton	1956 Diesel Electric	Taylor & Hubbard				
C 619	5 Ton	1914 Hand Trav	Cowan & Sheldon	Ex-M & GC No.1		1.1.55	2
C 620	5 Ton	1926 Steam Crane	Thomas Smith & Sons	Ex-T.W. Ward 6.2.58		4.83	
C 621	5 Ton	1935 Steam Crane	Thomas Smith & Sons	Ex-McAlpine 7.58		3.83	3
DEC 622	6 Ton	1964 Diesel Electric	Taylor & Hubbard				
C 623	7½ Ton	1982 Diesel	Cowan & Sheldon				
C 624	7½ Ton	1984 Diesel	Cowan & Sheldon				
C 625	7½ Ton	1984 Diesel	Cowan & Sheldon				
C 626	7½ Ton	1984 Diesel	Cowan & Sheldon				
C 627		1986 Diesel	Cowan & Sheldon				

NOTES
1 Converted to Diesel Operation by Cowan & Sheldon
2 To BR (LMR). Preserved at Quainton Road.
3 Preserved by Museum of London.
4 Received secondhand.
5 Secondhand Ex-T. Ward.

JIB CARRIERS

LT No.	Type		Built	Scrapped	Note
J 680	6 Ton	1897	Ex-MR Ballast Wagon No.5	1.7.62	
J 681	6 Ton	1882	Ex-MR Ballast Wagon No.42	30.4.47	
J 682	6 Ton	1886	Ex-MR Ballast Wagon No.50	22.5.68	1
J 683	8 Ton	1919	Ex-MR Service Stock No.14	1.6.65	
J 683		1937	Ex-WPW 1001 2.75	15.2.86	
J 684	8 Ton	1932	Ex-J174X 13.6.35 to J174	9.80	
J 685	8 Ton	1932	Ex-K175X 13.6.35 to J175	28.2.63	
J 686	10 Ton	1899	Ex-RW 450A 18.11.46	9.5.68	
J 687	10 Ton	1899	Ex-RW 450 B 18.11.46	9.5.68	
J 688	25 Ton	1925	Ex-F308 1.53	11.1.86	2
J 689	25 Ton	1925	Ex-F309 .55		
J 609	5 Ton	1914	Ex-MLGC No.1	1.1.55	
J 691	30 Ton	1931	Ex-F312 9.63		

1 Latterly used as accommodation wagon to hold steam engine boilers at Lillie Bridge.
2 Scrapped at Cockfosters by LUL.

GAUGING CARS

No.	Origin	Numbering History			Scrapped
G 660	1907 LER	(F124)	320 5.31	G 660 21.3.36	9.5.68
G 661	1919 CSLR	(G 206)		G 661 28.2.36	12.3.36
G 662	1906 MAR	Ex-CT 66 12.6.34 (G1)		G 662	9.80
G 663	1931 BRCW	Ex-7131		G 663 23.8.63	

RAIL GRINDING CARS

No.	Origin	Numbering History				Scrapped
RG 800	1906 LER	Ex-RG 207				21.6.55
RG 801	1906 ACF	Ex-1574 13.6.36 (Exhibition Car)				21.6.55
RG 802	1923 MCW	751 to 1751 .26	5241 4.35	75241 18.11.39	RG 802 4.9.56	29.11.85
RG 803	1923 MCW	755 to 1755 .26	5245 9.33	75245 2.1.39	RG 803 4.9.56	13.12.85

SLEET & DIESEL ELECTRIC LOCOS

LT No.	Origin	No.	Re-No.	Origins No.	Re-No.	LT Re-No.	Converted	Scrapped	Notes
ESL100	1903 BRCW	229	440 11.26	256	465 3.27	3960 1.34	22.12.38	14.10.82	1
ESL101	1903 MCW/BRCW	225	438 6.27	254	463 5.27	3958 12.33	16.11.39	25.4.84	
ESL102	1903 BRCW	261	470 4.27	267	477 7.27	3990 6.34	21.10.39	12.4.84	
ESL103	1903 BRCW	246	456 1.27	249	459 6.27	3976 4.33	21.11.39	11.5.54	2
ESL104	1903 BRCW	242	451 11.26	250	460 3.27	3971 10.34	11.11.39	13.4.84	
ESL105	1903 MCW/BRCW	219	432 6.27	236	445 10.26	3952 4.35	23.11.39	9.9.82	
ESL106	1903 BRCW	253	464 5.27	263	473 12.26	3984 12.34	29.11.39	13.4.84	
ESL107	1903 MCW/BRCW	208	424 12.26	252	461 2.27	3944 4.34	14.12.39		
ESL108	1903 BRCW	258	469 7.27	262	472 3.27	3989 7.33	23.12.39	12.4.84	
ESL109	1903 BRCW	237	448 8.27	241	452 11.26	3968 10.34	17.1.40	24.10.75	
ESL110	1903 BRCW	257	467 2.27	264	474 12.26	3987 9.34	14.2.40	28.10.75	
ESL111	1903 MCW	224	436 7.27	228	439 5.27	3956 3.35	28.2.40	16.9.82	
ESL112	1903 MCW	207	425 9.26	217	430 4.27	3945 6.34	29.3.40	6.81	
ESL113	1903 BRCW	230	442 4.27	240	449 1.27	3962 7.33	16.4.40	19.7.80	
ESL114	1903 BRCW	238	447 11.26	239	450 10.26	3967 8.34	11.5.40	26.4.84	
ESL115	1903 BRCW	251	462 8.27	260	471 3.27	3982 1.35	30.5.40	24.10.75	
ESL116	1903 MCW/BRCW	218	433 5.27	234	444 7.27	3953 7.33	21.6.40	12.10.82	
ESL117	1903 MCW/BRCW	223	434 3.27	265	475 4.27	3954 10.34	19.7.40		
ESL118A	1933 BRCW	258				2758	17.4.61		
ESL118B	1933 BRCW	249				2749	17.4.61		
DEL120	1903 MAR	226	294 10.25	212	298 12.25	3937 5.34	24.7.41	11.7.58	3
			417 8.27		421 8.27				

NOTES
1 Prototype Conversion   2 Collision 2.53   3 To Electric Loco 5.11.55

STORES CARS

No.	Origin	Orig.No.	Re-No.	Later Re-numberings	LT Re-No.	Converted	Scrapped
SC630	1888	Ex-MR covered van No.1					11.7.58
SC631	1902	Ex-MR LSO 398					11.7.58
SC632	1903 BRCW	Ex-MR milk van No.6					11.7.58
SC633	1905 Ivry	424	1256 2.28		SC66 6.30	SC201 5.31	SC633 2.36	27.4.38
SC634	1905 Ivry	415	1249 11.29		SC67 6.30	SC202 5.31	SC634 2.36	27.4.38
SC635	1905 Ivry	412	1246		SC68 6.30	SC203 5.31	SC635 2.36	27.4.38
SC636	1905 Ivry	416	1250		SC69 6.30	SC204 5.31	SC636 2.36	27.4.38
SC637	1913 GRCW	568	229 8.29 4139 12.34				SC637 7.58	7.3.63
SC638	1910 H-Nelson	180	111 7.29 4011 9.33 4214 7.38				SC638 7.58	7.3.63
SC639	1910 H-Nelson	550	145 10.29 4045 9.33				SC639 7.58	6.7.67
SC640	1910 H-Nelson	200	131 3.28 4031 5.33 8901 12.50				SC640 7.58	7.3.63

BRAKE VANS

No.		Origin		Capacity	Scrapped
B 550	1890	MCW	Ex-DR B199	9 Tons	9.12.40
B 551	1890	MCW	Ex-MR Ballast Brake No.4	11 Tons	29.5.50
B 552	1890	MCW	Ex-MR Ballast Brake No.5	11 Tons	2.11.69
B 553	1914	MCW	Ex-MR Ballast Brake No.24	13 Tons	2.11.69
B 554	1914	MCW	Ex-MR Ballast Brake No.25	13 Tons	2.11.69
B 555	1935	Hurst Nelson B 220		20 Tons	18.5.84
B 556	1935	Hurst Nelson B 221		20 Tons	
B 557	1935	Hurst Nelson B 222		20 Tons	10.81
B 558	1935	Hurst Nelson B 223		20 Tons	
B 559	1935	Hurst Nelson B 224		20 Tons	18.5.84
B 560	1935	Hurst Nelson B 225		20 Tons	
B 561	1887		Ex-MR Ballast Brake No.1	10 Tons	1.7.62
B 562	1893		Ex-MR Ballast Brake No.8	10 Tons	1.7.62
B 563	1895		Ex-MR Ballast Brake No.14	10 Tons	28.3.61
B 564	1894		Ex-MR Ballast Brake No.12	10 Tons	2.11.69
B 565	1894		Ex-MR Ballast Brake No.13	10 Tons	1.7.62
B 566	1895		Ex-MR Ballast Brake No.16	10 Tons	14.3.68
B 567	1895		Ex-MR Ballast Brake No.15	10 Tons	14.3.68
B 568					
B 569	1895		Ex-MR Ballast Brake No.17	10 Tons	28.3.61
B 570					
B 571					
B 572	1896		Ex-MR Ballast Brake No.20	10 Tons	14.3.68
B 573	1896		Ex-MR Ballast Brake No.21	10 Tons	28.3.61
B 574	1896		Ex-MR Ballast Brake No.22	10 Tons	10.1.52
B 575	1896		Ex-MR Ballast Brake No.23	10 Tons	2.11.69
B 576	1901		Ex-MR Pass'gr Brake No.5		29.11.39
B 577	1901		Ex-MR Pass'gr Brake No.6	10 Tons	11.7.58
FB 578	1935	GRCW	Ex-F330 5.50	18 Tons	28.6.84
FB 579	1935	GRCW	Ex-F327 6.50	18 Tons	16.12.83
B 580	1962	BR Ashford	To Tube Match Wagon	20 Tons	
B 581	1962	BR Ashford		20 Tons	
B 582	1962	BR Ashford		20 Tons	
B 583	1962	BR Ashford	To Surface Match Wagon	20 Tons	
B 584	1962	BR Ashford	To Surface Match Wagon	20 Tons	
B 585	1962	BR Ashford	To Tube Match Wagon	20 Tons	

568/70/71 were to have been Ex-MR Goods Brakes, sold to LNER 1.11.37

TANK WAGON

No.	Entered Service		Scrapped
TW 730	28.1.33	Ex Stores Car of DR Origin	9.80

BREAKDOWN VANS

No.	Origin		Re-Numberings		Scrapped
BDV 700	1896 BRCW	Ex-MR Milk Van No.3	BD 221 24.11.34	BDV 700 31.12.37	19.7.65
BDV 701	1903 Neasden	Ex-MR Milk Van No.5	BD 220 14.9.34	BDV 701 31.12.37	19.6.44
BDV 702	1899	Ex-MR Service Stock No.1		BDV 702 31.12.37	19.7.65
BDV 703	1910	Ex-MR Service Stock No.2		BDV 703 31.12.37	19.7.65
BDV 704	1910	Ex-MR Service Stock No.3		BDV 704 31.12.37*	26.10.56

*Previously renumbered BW251 on 31.8.37

BREAKDOWN WAGON

No.	Built			Scrapped
BDW 704	1897	Ex-BW 195 22.2.46		19.7.65

INSTRUCTION CARS

No.	Origin	Numbering History					Scrapped
IC 1075	1920 CL	700 1700 .26	2043 5.30	5170 7.34	IC 1075 15.11.49		14.5.69
IC 1076	1920 CL	817	1333 5.30	7243 6.35	IC 1076 15.11.49		14.5.69
IC 1077	1920 CL	802	1318 5.30	7248 6.35	IC 1077 15.11.49		14.5.69
IC 1078	1920 CL	815	1331 5.30	7241 6.35	IC 1078 15.11.49		14.5.69
IC 1079	1920 CL	809	1325 5.30	7235 6.35	IC 1079 15.11.49		14.5.69

PERSONNEL CARRIERS

No.	Origin		Numbering History					Scrapped
PC 850	1931 BRCW	7061				PC 850	4.1.65	
PC 851	1931 BRCW	7063				PC 851	4.1.65	
PC 852	1931 BRCW	7080				PC 852	25.10.66	
PC 853	1931 BRCW	7114				PC 853	25.10.66	4.12.72
PC 854	1931 GRCW	7158				PC 854	12.11.66	12.10.84
PC 855	1931 BRCW	7071				PC 855	22.11.66	
PC 856	1927 MCW	1168	7518	4.35	70518 16.1.39	PC 856	7.72	4.5.84
PC 857	1938 MCW	11247				PC 857	11.80	
PC 858	1938 MCW	11165				PC 858	12.80	
PC 859	1938 MCW	10165				PC 859	2.81	

WEED KILLER CARS

No.	Origin	Numbering History						Scrapped
WK 840	1905 Brush	DM 55	DM 8	2.30	WK 214 25.3.35	WK 840		27.2.50
WK 841	1905 MAR	T 362	CT 1712	2.30	WK 215 18.5.35	WK 841		4.3.38
WK 842	1905 Brush	DM 10			WK 842 24.3.37			27.2.50

DIESEL GENERATOR WAGON

No.	Origin	Converted to
WPW 1000	27.12.37 Acton Works	Bogie Well Wagon 1.75

WELL WAGON FOR DIESEL GENERATOR WAGON

No.	Origin	Converted to
WPW 1001	8.9.37 Acton Works	JC 683 2.75

CABLE DRUM WAGONS

No.	Origin
CW 1050	1.3.40 GRCW
CW 1051	1.3.40 GRCW
CW 1052	1.3.40 GRCW

COAL ELEVATOR WAGON

No.	Origin	Scrapped
CE 740	1910 Ex-MR Service Stock No.12 12.37	4.3.42
CE 741	1910 Ex-MR Service Stock No.13 12.37	4.3.42

WEIGHING MACHINE ADJUSTMENT VANS

No.	Origin	Scrapped
TV 750	1910 Ex-MR Service Stock No.6 12.37	12.3.43
TV 751	1910 Ex-MR Service Stock No.7 12.37	7.4.44

TUNNEL LINE CLEANING WAGONS

No	Origin	Scrapped
TLC1	1904 Ex-BW108 6.48	16.9.78
TLC2	1893 Ex-BW248 6.48	16.9.78

SLEET WAGONS

No.	Origin			Re-Numbered	Scrapped
SW 810	1881 Ashbury	8-Wheel 3rd CL	Ex-MR 213		8.10.41
SW 811	1883 Brown Marshall	8-Wheel 3rd CL	Ex-MR 226		30.8.41
SW 812	1883 Brown Marshall	8-Wheel 3rd CL	Ex-MR 236		30.8.41
SW 813	1884 Brown Marshall	8-Wheel 2nd CL	Ex-MR 300		30.8.51
SW 814A	1925		Ex-LER 37/71	SW 191	28.6.39
SW 814B	1925			SW 193	28.6.39
SW 815	1927 BRCW		Ex-LER 316	SW 192	23.4.40
SW 816	1933 Acton			SW 213	18.6.40
SW 817	1933 Acton			SW 211	28.1.43
SW 818	1933 Acton			SW 212	6.9.43
PSW 819	1938 Acton				1.1.43

SLEET TENDERS

No.	Origin	Scrapped
ST 1	1.1.1957 Acton Works	17.10.60
ST 2	31.1.1957 Acton Works	17.10.60

SUMMARY OF OTHER WAGONS

BW1-266	Ballast Wagons	RW801-826	Rail Wagons
HW201-222	Hopper Wagons	HD871-876	High Deck Wagons
F300-398	Flat Wagons	*PH/SL/A 901-982	Power House, Slurry and Ash Wagons
HW400-437	Hopper Wagons	GP901-941	General Purpose Wagons
RW450-506	Rail Wagons		
MW500-543	Match Wagons	*Not all numbers in this series were used	